CLASS CONFLICT AND COALITION IN THE CALIFORNIA WOMAN SUFFRAGE MOVEMENT 1907 - 1912

The San Francisco Wage Earners' Suffrage League

CLASS CONFLICT AND COALITION IN THE CALIFORNIA WOMAN SUFFRAGE MOVEMENT 1907 - 1912

The San Francisco Wage Earners' Suffrage League

Susan Englander

The Edwin Mellen Press
Lewiston/Queenston/Lampeter

Library of Congress Cataloging-in-Publication Data

Englander, Susan.
    Class conflict and class coalition in the California woman
suffrage movement, 1907 - 1912 : the San Francisco Wage Earners'
Suffrage League / Susan Englander.
     p.   cm.
    Includes bibliographical references and index.
    ISBN 0-7734-9845-1
    1. Women--Suffrage--California--San Francisco--History. 2. San
Francisco Wage Earners' Suffrage League--History. 3. Women in trade
-unions--California--San Francisco--History. 4. Social conflict-
-California--San Francisco--History. I. Title.
JK1911.C2E54 1992
324.6'23'0979461--dc20   91-39312
                                                  CIP

A CIP catalog record for this book
is available from the British Library.

The Edwin Mellen Press   The Edwin Mellen Press
Box 450   Box 67
Lewiston, New York   Queenston, Ontario
USA 14092   CANADA L0S 1L0

The Edwin Mellen Press, Ltd.
Lampeter, Dyfed, Wales
UNITED KINGDOM SA48 7DY

Printed in the United States of America

To my mother,
Justine R. Englander

TABLE OF CONTENTS

List of Tables iii

Foreword v

Acknowledgements vii

Introduction 1

Chapter 1 - "Yes, We Are Politicians": San Francisco Woman Unionists
and Feminism, 1900-1911 15

Chapter 2 - Fighting for Justice Versus Searching for Order: Class
Conflict in the California Woman Suffrage Movement,
1896-1909 73

Chapter 3 - "To Secure the Labor Vote": Union Women and the "Last
Push" for Woman Suffrage in California 109

Aftermath and Conclusions - "This Newer and Larger Woman's
Movement" 157

Selected Bibliography 179

Index 189

LIST OF TABLES

Table 1:   Nativity of All San Francisco Residents, 1910 18

Table 2:   San Francisco Foreign-Born White Stock, 1900 and 1910 19

Table 3:   Nativity of San Francisco Wage-Earning Women, 1910 21

Table 4:   Parentage of San Francisco Working Women, 1900 24

Table 5:   San Francisco Wage-Earning Women, 1890-1910 27

Table 6:   Residential Status of San Francisco Wage-Earning
Women, 1900 29

Table 7:   Ages of SF Wage-Earning Women Living Apart from
Family, 1900 29

Table 8:   Nativity of SF Female Wage-Earners Living Away from
Home, 1900 29

Table 9:   Ages of San Francisco Wage-Earning Women, 1900 31

Table 10: Marital Status of San Francisco Wage-Earning Women, 1990 . 34

Table 11: Most Common Women's Occupations: San Francisco 1910 . . 36

Table 12: Women's Job Categories - San Francisco 1910 37

Table 13: San Francisco Female Union Membership, 1913 44

Table 14: San Francisco Election Results: Amendment Eight 138

Table 15: Votes for Amendment Eight Compared to Total Vote, 1911 . 139

Table 16: San Francisco Election Results: 1896 and 1911 Woman
Suffrage Amendments 142

Table 17: San Francisco Female Voting Registration, FY 1912-1912 . . 161

Table 18: Comparison of Female Registration to Female Population
in San Francisco by Neighborhood, FY 1912-1913 162

FOREWORD

REHEARSAL FOR REFORM

by

Frances Richardson Keller

At some time every student must have wondered at the slight treatment of women's struggles in history texts: Where is the drama, the bitter disappointment, the sudden insight, the crisis moment, the whole luxuriant spectacle attendant to all human happenings?

In The San Francisco Wage Earners' Suffrage League, Susan L. Englander details -- for the first time -- the complexities of "class conflict and class coalition" that characterized the California Woman Suffrage Movement of the years 1907 to 1912. That movement produced a preview; it staged a rehearsal for events to come. Like all rehearsals, it carried within itself the dangers and the triumphs attendant to change.

Focusing upon class differences, Susan Englander shows exactly and minutely how that movement in California furnishes an introduction to national accommodations crucial to women's advancement. Englander traces evolutionary dynamics in the development of leadership and in membership positions in California women's organizations; she shows the efforts, the growth of individuals; she shows the tactics later leaders would need to understand and to adopt or reject. She shows the defeats and the successes that form the story of the San Francisco Wage Earners Suffrage League.

She shows what it took to reach the goals these women set. In filling out the picture, she describes little known women union members and union officers, -- like Maud Younger, Louise La Rue, Minna O'Donnell -- as well as middle class women reformers, -- like Gail Laughlin, Lillian Harris Coffin, Mary Sperry, Ellen Clark Sargent. These women and many others lived with deprivations of differing dimensions. But all of them shared a vision.

Englander tells the story of their efforts to understand and to accommodate one another, beset as they were by clashing backgrounds, family demands, cultural and economic and personal prohibitions. Able women whose achievements have rested in obscurity emerge in this light; working women whose lives have provided the backbone of civilized society come into view. Naturally, these people chose different ways to express dissatisfactions. In this study, we see that variations in culture, in resources, in life experiences made coming together extremely difficult. But all of them desired a nourishing, equitable, less violent, less polarized society. There were tales of striking ingenuity. There were setbacks, there were successes. Strangely, we still scarcely recognize the names of the women whose actions moved enormous obstacles.

In addition, most of the women were little concerned to provide the personal recollections historians cherish. While some of Englander's material came fortuitously to her attention, most of the substance which informs her study required patient search. It required ingenious piecing together of materials. The study therefore provides a model. It demonstrates that in the hands of a creative scholar the fuller story can come to life. We can see its meaning.

The study demonstrates that we can retrieve much of the richness of women's histories, and that what we retrieve can be as respectable as any histories. Above all, Englander's study demonstrates that the effort is worth the trouble. Without doubt this study yields a fairer, fuller understanding of human happenings.

ACKNOWLEDGEMENTS

While writing history ultimately rests with one person, she must depend on the skills and good will of others to get the job done well. I would first like to thank Robert W. Cherny, Jules Tygiel and Frances Richardson Keller, the tireless members of my thesis committee who proved the axiom that busy people are the most productive ones. In addition, it was through Professor Keller's encouragement and efforts that this project became a book. Her support has been a model for me of sisterhood and collegiality.

I began this study in 1986, the seventy-fifth anniversary of women's enfranchisement in California. Lyn Bonfield, director of the Labor Archives and Research Center at San Francisco State University, helped initiate this project and Dorothy Sue Cobble, then director of Labor Studies at City College, San Francisco, confirmed that the WESL was worth investigating. I thank them both for that initial spark of inspiration and encouragement. Thanks also go to Janet Lenore Pigniolo, Kathleen Brown, Nina Jo Smith, Cita Cook, Barbara Byrd and Rochelle Gatlin, who read and commented on the drafts of chapters; Sherry Katz, who shared her research on Frances Noel with me; Philip Ethington, for his contribution on gender and politics; Deborah Brudno, who did indispensable work for me in the Library of Congress; Nancy Breen, for her insights on race and San Francisco labor; Ruth Shackelford, whose database on San Francisco female workers in 1900 proved to be essential; Jeanne McDonnell, for sharing her research on California suffrage; Barbara Grey, for her work on early San Francisco female printers; Rebecca Mead, whose subsequent work on San Francisco female wage-earners and enduring enthusiasm gave me much needed intellectual support and energy during some difficult times; Kathleen Farmer, whose presence always reinvigorated me and whose recent death deeply saddened me; Melanie Curtis, whose patience and technical expertise has made this book a reality; and to Mike Pincus, whose valuable editorial contributions in the home stretch made an enormous difference. The students and faculty of the San Francisco State University History Department from 1984-89 provided me with a creative and lively environment in which to study and write; thanks to you all.

I am also indebted to the Bay Area Labor History Workshop, which provided me with the first place to publicly present my work on the WESL, and offered friendly and constructive criticism to a fledgling scholar.

My work was made less stressful through the generous efforts of the librarians and archivists I encountered in the course of my research. Thanks go to the staffs of the J. Paul Leonard Library at San Francisco State University, the Sutro Library, the San Francisco Public Library, the California Historical Society, the Chancery Archives of the Archdiocese of San Francisco, the California State Library, the Special Collections Room at the UCLA Research Library, the Huntington Library, the Sophia Smith Collection at Smith College, the Arthur and Elizabeth Schlesinger Library on the History of Women in America at Radcliffe College, the Holt-Atherton Center for Western History at the University of the Pacific, and the Library of Congress.

I owe an inestimable debt to my colleagues in the feminist and labor movements. Our discussions, disagreements and queries on the past and present conditions of social change led me back to graduate school to study these questions in a more systematic and thoughtful way. Their contributions and lives have enriched this study beyond measure.

Finally, I would like to give a special thanks to John Durham, companion, co-conspirator and inveterate punster, who saw this project through with me, and got me into and out of some very ticklish situations.

INTRODUCTION

For California suffragists, October 12, 1911 was a day of rejoicing. The state's male electorate added Amendment Eight to the state constitution, granting women the right to vote. With that act, California became the sixth state to give women total suffrage rights. This hard-won victory climaxed a forty-two year effort by state suffragists to win for women the political right to participate as full voting citizens.[1]

California's final campaign has received surprisingly little attention, considering that this victory appears to have been a major turning point in the national fight for the enfranchisement of women. In the few accounts available, suffragists are uniformly depicted as middle-class women.[2]

This picture perpetuates a common fallacy--that working class and trade union women did not participate in the fight for suffrage and indeed opposed giving women the right to vote. According to Ellen Carol DuBois, "characterizing the early twentieth-century suffrage movement as middle-class obscures its most striking element, the new interest in the vote among women at both ends of the class structure. Furthermore, it tends to homogenize the movement."[3] Particularly in San Francisco, female wage earners were actively involved in the final phase of the campaign for woman suffrage, verbalized prosuffrage opinions publicly, formed an organization to promote the suffrage cause, successfully lobbied labor organizations to support suffrage actively and worked side by side with middle-class suffragists to ensure passage of Amendment Eight.

San Francisco union women founded the Wage Earners' Suffrage League (WESL) as the vehicle for their suffrage involvement. The WESL provided these union feminists a place to develop their own leaders and pro-suffrage strategy in a separate, autonomous organization which recognized and spoke to the class differences between these women and their middle-class counterparts. The WESL received official sanction by the San Francisco labor movement for its activities and was accepted as an official union organization by the San Francisco Labor Council in its drive to "secure the labor vote."[4]

Finally, the WESL's existence depended heavily on an upper-middle-class ally of union women, Maud Younger. Younger's political acumen, wealth, bounty of free time, and sense of kinship with union and wage-earning women proved to be invaluable to the WESL and its leadership. These assets sustained the organization while union women remained active in their unions, served on the Labor Council and its committees, and performed their jobs. Younger and the union suffragists of the WESL were full participants in the final campaign for woman suffrage in California. Their involvement left its mark on both the labor and suffrage movements, as well as the women themselves.

The WESL arose in an era now known for its high level of female activism. Temperance, civil rights for Blacks, settlement work, higher education, and municipal reform all involved women as both leaders and foot soldiers in the national experience known as Progressivism.[5]

Included in this panoply of issues and organizations was the women's trade union movement. While they experienced many fits and starts during the nineteenth century, labor organizations with, of, and for women truly came into their own at this time, emerging as stable and on-going entities able to represent women in the workplace.

Like many reformist efforts, the women's labor movement concerned itself with the well-being of women, especially on the job. Unionists fought for shorter work days and better pay, for safer, healthier, and more comfortable work areas, and for specific job descriptions. In the process, they learned to organize around specific goals and demands, developed speaking skills, and began to articulate a shared body of interests for working women, all faculties analogous to those arising among middle-class suffragists as a result of their political activities. At the same time, working with middle-class feminists exposed them to an ideology of gender equality and justice.

It should be no surprise that at the turn of the century women trade unionists began to demonstrate an interest in political strategies in general, and the vote in particular, as ways to entrench their gains and to make further inroads as workers and as women. This was particularly true in San Francisco where unionism secured a voice in city politics and "[held] undisputed sway" through the triumph of the Union Labor Party in most municipal elections from 1901 through 1909.[6]

This book chronicles the brief existence of the San Francisco Wage Earners' Suffrage League. The first chapter describes the situation of San Francisco's female work force and unions, and the historical circumstances which produced the WESL's union activists. Chapter two is devoted to the split between union and reform suffragists which resulted in the formation of the WESL. The final chapter chronicles the WESL's history as an organization and its contribution to the 1911 victorious campaign for woman suffrage, including that of its union leadership and of Maud Younger. Its thesis reflects the current synthesis of two major areas of historical research--the woman suffrage movement and the lives of wage-earning women, particularly in the Progressive

Era. These two fields emerged as a part of the "new history" which focuses on the lives of ordinary people as well as the institutions and organizations that affected their lives.

The suffragists themselves wrote the first histories of the struggle for women's enfranchisement. Beginning with Susan B. Anthony and Elizabeth Cady Stanton's collaboration on the first volume of History of Woman Suffrage, veterans of the movement produced numerous accounts filled with first-hand experiences and observations. These works continued to appear through the 1960s.[7]

General histories of the Progressive Era, on the other hand, have usually contained one obligatory reference to woman suffrage. This approach drained the movement of any notion of breadth and depth, and negated the role many suffragists played in other organizations and coalitions.[8] The few full-length treatments of the woman suffrage movement portrayed it as isolated and limited. Its activists, these works implied, operated in a kind of a vacuum, caring only for the vote and disengaged from other concerns of the era.[9]

Only Eleanor Flexner's detailed and broad history of the movement, Century of Struggle, avoided these flaws. Demonstrating that pro-suffrage support and activity came from many diverse sources, Flexner blended the histories of white and black abolitionists, wage-earners, clubwomen, settlement house workers, and educators along with the story of specific suffrage organizations into a complex and generous history of the seventy-year long effort. Dedicated to her suffragist mother, Century of Struggle appeared in the late 1950s, but initially received scant attention or recognition.[10]

The history of woman suffrage fell into disfavor during the early 1970s because historians of women and their readers criticized those studies which defined "the only women whose lives are worth recording" as those who "gained recognition by succeeding in overcoming institutional obstacles . . . in a framework of accomplishment defined by men."[11] A new school of woman's history burgeoned in these years, nourished by the exuberant women's liberation movement. These historians disowned a narrow focus on suffrage as "archaic and fairly useless"[12] and turned instead to the study of women's daily lives or women's culture.[13] Many turned their attention to the lives of women working both within the confines of the home as well as in the labor force. They redefined the term "work" itself, maintaining that many forms of labor, such as housekeeping and child-rearing, had gone unrecognized and uncredited for centuries.[14]

By 1980, Ellen Carol DuBois challenged this retreat from political history, concerned that "questions of culture have come to replace questions of politics." This shift, she maintained, transformed women's history into something "'depoliticized' and academic in the worst sense of the word" and DuBois called for a return to a more political focus with an emphasis on social change.[15]

Historians answered DuBois's call with a spate of studies which detailed overt, institutional political activity as well as the political dimensions of women's lives that lay unrevealed when traditional definitions of "politics" informed historical analysis.[16] In this more receptive environment, suffrage history returned to prominence, but as a different and more complex subject. While some scholars investigated suffrage organizations,[17] others focused their attention on the state campaigns for women's enfranchisement and their aftermath.[18]

The current synthesis, heralded by Susan Reverby's article "The Labor and Suffrage Movements," published in 1969, boasts such efforts as Meredith Tax's The Rising of the Women, depicting the militancy of Progressive Era wage-earning women, Nancy Schrom Dye's book on the New York chapter of the Women's Trade Union League, As Equals and as Sisters, Diane Balser's examination of several working-class women's organizations in Sisterhood and

Solidarity, and Ellen Carol DuBois's prize-winning story of Harriot Stanton Blatch and the Equality League for Self-Supporting Women.[19] Each of these works acknowledges the connection between wage-earning women, women who work outside of the home for pay, and political processes. Indeed, the women depicted in these books consciously realized their interest in political activity and involvement in the workings of the state.

Most recently, Nancy Cott's study, The Grounding of Modern Feminism provides another point of perspective for those interested in progressivism and suffrage to view the mobilization of union women on behalf of their own enfranchisement. Cott credits the emergence of a modern brand of feminism, distinct from and broader than the nineteenth-century "woman movement," with "encouraging into voice women who spoke out not only about disenfranchisement by sex, but about disenfranchisement explicitly informed by racial, political, or economic loyalties: black women, white southern women, socialist women, trade union women." This was possible, Cott asserts, due to feminism's emphasis on individual rights and, therefore, the recognition of diversity among women versus its former adherence to a universal and uniform conception of "woman." The development of this eclectic concept permitted middle-class suffragists to see their working-class counterparts as deserving of the vote. In turn, a notion of individual rights helped wage-earning women to understand that woman suffrage could serve their interests. This recognition, and the circumstances surrounding San Francisco's suffrage movement, inspired the formation of an organization of female unionists devoted to the cause of suffrage.[20]

It was no coincidence that the bulk of these working-class activists cut their organizational teeth through participation in their unions, usually as organizers or officers. Wage work itself was not enough of a catalyst to guarantee a conversion to the suffrage cause. As a matter of fact, Leslie Tentler, Susan Estabrook Kennedy and Sarah Eisenstein demonstrated exactly the opposite -- that women's wage work at the turn of the century often mirrored and reinforced the subordinate position of women in the home, serving to encourage women's passivity and noninvolvement in the public sphere.[21]

As early as the Progressive Era, Lillian Matthews, who studied economics at the University of California at Berkeley, had noted in her 1913 dissertation on women in San Francisco labor unions that unionism served "as an educational stimulant. . . . At her meetings the trade union member must accustom herself to expressing her opinions. This drill develops a poise and self-confidence which makes it easier to face situations outside of union halls. . . . Experience in contesting for their rights in union halls seems to have developed leaders among the trade union women."[22] In a culture which still frowned upon women's public activity, trade unions molded wage-earning women into social and political activists. In San Francisco, where unions had direct access to City Hall during most of twentieth century's first decade, it was a significant step to involvement in the movement to grant women the ballot.

The San Francisco Wage Earners' Suffrage League and its activists, viewed in this perspective, was one of the "scores of aggressive, politically active pressure groups" that Daniel Rodgers described in his ground-breaking article, "In Search of Progressivism." Rodgers commented that the latest wave of histories on the Progressive Era emphasized the pluralism and diversity of that period's myriad organizations and movements, instead of seeking to find the essential values and goals which united them. In this context, woman suffrage can be explored as a movement within an era of movements.[23]

In the early 1900s, working class women became an element within the woman suffrage movement when they recognized the value of the ballot. For the purposes of this study, these women will be referred to as wage-earners i.e., women employed for pay and compensated at an hourly, daily or piece rate, differentiating them from professional women who receive a salary as well as from those who keep house, raise children, or participate in a family business without remuneration.   Simultaneously, middle-class suffragists realized the importance of the working-class vote in winning the statewide contests for women's enfranchisement, and regarded alliances with these women as a means of securing those votes.

The subjects of this study were not only exclusively white, but part of a white worker's movement which sought to assert itself at the expense of California's Asian workers.   Their race, then, is not merely a fact to be acknowledged but a factor in the formation of these women's institutions and consciousness.

Linda Kerber and Jane De Hart-Mathews observe that historians must regard "women's experience as basic, not incidental, to how we view the past," particularly the Progressive Era.   They propose that scholars perceive progressivism as part of women's history.   In addition, they posit that male reformers appropriated from female activists the ideas which lay at the core of the Progressive spirit, particularly those associated with social justice and social control.   They often promoted these causes as their own, denying women credit and leadership in the process.   This "refocusing" on women and gender, as Kerber and De Hart-Mathews termed it, allows the era's female reformers and activists stature comparable to those men already recognized as integral to the period's documentation and recognizes the multiplicity of women's organizations and intentions.   In redirecting our gaze to women who have, until recently, remained in the background of history, we must further adjust our sights to encompass the experiences and organizations of working-class women.[24]

The San Francisco Wage Earners' Suffrage League was such an organization.   An association of politically-conscious trade union women, its presence reflected the inter-class tensions between these women and their reform-minded counterparts, and established the significance of working-class women's contribution to the suffrage movement.

NOTES TO INTRODUCTION

1.   California suffragists founded the first organization to win the franchise, the California Woman Suffrage Association, in 1869. Donald Waller Rodes, "The California Woman Suffrage Campaign of 1911" (M.A. thesis, California State University, Hayward, 1974), 4.

2.   Mrs. Robert La Follette, and others, "Six Months of Suffrage in California," West Coast Magazine 12 (July 1912), 419-438; Selina Solomons, How We Won the Vote in California: A True Story of the Campaign of 1911 (San Francisco: The New Woman Publishing Co., n.d.); Ida Husted Harper, The History of Woman Suffrage, Volume 6, 1900-1920 (New York: National American Woman Suffrage Association, 1922), 27-58.

3.   Ellen Carol DuBois, "Working Women, Class Relations, and Suffrage Militance: Harriot Stanton Blatch and the New York Woman Suffrage Movement, 1894-1909," Journal of American History 74 (June 1987): 35.

4.   Selina Solomons, How We Won the Vote in California: A True Story of the Campaign of 1911 (San Francisco: The New Woman Publishing Co., n.d.), 25.

5.   See Stephen M. Buechler, The Transformation of the Woman Suffrage Movement: The Case of Illinois, 1850-1920 (New Brunswick: Rutgers University Press, 1986) and Felice D. Gordon, After Winning: The Legacy of New Jersey Suffragists (New Brunswick: Rutgers University Press, 1985) for two good examples of suffrage documentation on the state level. For information on temperance, see Ruth Bordin, Women and Temperance (Philadelphia: Temple University Press, 1981). For a history of the settlement house movement, see Allen F. Davis, Spearheads For Reform: The Social Settlements and the Progressive Movement, 1890-1914 (New Brunswick: Rutgers University Press, 1984).   For a thorough treatment of black women and suffrage, see Paula Giddings, When and Where I Enter (New York: William Morrow & Co., 1984; New York: Bantam Books, 1984). Arthur S. Link and Richard L. McCormick, Progressivism (Arlington Heights, IL: Harlan Davidson, Inc., 1983), provides a good overview of the constituent elements of Progressivism. See Linda K. Kerber and Jane De Hart-Mathews, Woman's America: Refocusing the Past (New York: Oxford University Press, 1987), 220-321, for documents and articles in all of these areas.

6.   The phrase, "where labor holds undisputed sway," comes from an article by Ray Stannard Baker, "A Corner in Labor: What Is Happening in San

Francisco Where Unionism Holds Undisputed Sway," McClure's 22 (February 1904): 366-378.

7.   Susan B. Anthony, Matilda Joslyn Gage, and others, History of Woman Suffrage, 4 vols. (Rochester, N.Y.: Susan B. Anthony, 1881-1902), vols. 5-6 (New York: National American Woman Suffrage Association, 1922); Harriot Stanton Blatch and Alma Lutz, Challenging Years: The Memoirs of Harriot Stanton Blatch (New York: G.P. Putnam & Sons, 1940); Inez Haynes Irwin, "Uphill With Banners Flying" (Penobscot, ME: Traversity Press, 1964). For a more detailed discussion of the early historiography of woman suffrage, see Ellen Carol DuBois, "Making Women's History: Activist Historians of Women's Rights, 1880-1940," Radical History Review (No. 49, Winter 1991): 61-84.

8.   Richard Hofstadter, The Age of Reform (New York: Vintage Books, 1955); Robert H. Wiebe, The Search for Order, 1877-1920 (New York: Hill and Wang, 1967); George E. Mowry, The California Progressives (Berkeley and Los Angeles: University of California Press, 1951).

9.   William L. O'Neill, Everyone Was Brave: The Rise and Fall of Feminism in America (Chicago: Quadrangle Press, 1969); Aileen S. Kraditor, The Ideas of the Woman Suffrage Movement (New York: Columbia University Press, 1965). J. Stanley Lemons extended this analysis of feminism into the 1920s; J. Stanley Lemons, The Woman Citizen: Social Feminism in the 1920s (Urbana and Chicago: University of Illinois Press, 1973). For a criticism of the dichotomous framework used to categorize early modern feminism in these books, see Nancy F. Cott, "What's in a Name? The Limits of 'Social Feminism'; or, Expanding the Vocabulary of Women's History," Journal of American History 76 (December 1989): 809-829.

10.   Eleanor Flexner, Century of Struggle (Cambridge: Harvard University Press, 1959; New York: Atheneum, 1973). Carol Lasser recently reappraised Flexner's contribution and concluded that "there is still no volume to rival Century of Struggle for its comprehensive analysis of who marshalled which forces and how in the woman suffrage movement, particularly in its last dozen years." Carol Lasser, "Century of Struggle, Decades of Revision: a Retrospective on Eleanor Flexner's Suffrage History," Reviews in American History 15 (June 1987): 344-354, 350.

11.   Lasser, "Century of Struggle, Decades of Revision," 350. Interestingly, Lasser drew this quote from a review of Century of Struggle published in 1975 in the Vassar College Miscellany News.

12.   Gerda Lerner, The Majority Finds Its Past: Placing Women in History (New York: Oxford University Press, 1979), 6. The chapter containing this quote originally appeared as an article in The Journal for Social History 3 (Fall 1969), 53-62.

13.   The classic study in this field is Carroll Smith-Rosenberg, "The Female World of Love and Rituals: Relations Between Women in Nineteenth-Century America," Signs 1 (Autumn 1975): 1-29.

14.   Lerner, The Majority Finds Its Past; Barbara Mayer Wertheimer, We Were There: The Story of Working Women in America (New York: Pantheon Books, 1977); Thomas Dublin, Women at Work: The Transformation of Work and Community in Lowell, Massachusetts, 1826-1860 (New York: Columbia University Press, 1979); Susan Estabrook Kennedy, If All We Did Was To Weep At Home: A History of White Working-Class Women In America (Bloomington: Indiana University Press, 1979); Leslie Woodcock Tentler, Wage-Earning Women: Industrial Work and Family Life in the United States, 1900-1930 (New York: Oxford University Press, 1979); Mary Ryan, Womanhood in America: From Colonial Times to the Present (New York: Franklin Watts, 1983); Philip Foner, Women and the American Labor Movement, 2 vols. (New York: The Free Press, 1979).

15.   Ellen Carol DuBois, Mari Jo Buhle, et al., "Politics and Culture in Women's History: A Symposium" Feminist Studies 6 (Spring 1980): 33, 34. DuBois' essay provoked a heated exchange in the pages of Feminist Studies. Mari Jo Buhle, a historian of woman and socialism, essentially agreed with DuBois. Gerda Lerner chided DuBois on playing fast and loose with her terminology and definitions and took a middle-ground position, stressing the merits of both types of history. Temma Kaplan, a Europeanist, reminded DuBois that class relations as well as politics must be central to the analysis of women's history. Finally, Carroll Smith-Rosenberg staunchly defended her advocacy of women's cultural history, maintaining that a woman-identified culture stood at the heart of the development of feminism and its politics. I would recommend these essays highly as an example of the thoughtfulness and depth of current women's history as well as proof that women's historians are not chips off the same block. DuBois had already demonstrated her commitment to a merger of women's history and politics with Feminism and Suffrage: The Emergence of an Independent Women's Movement In America, 1848-1869 (Ithaca: Cornell University Press, 1978). This debate also took place in the historical community at large and is reflected in Thomas Bender's call for a synthesis of political and social history; Thomas Bender, "Wholes and Parts: The

Need for Synthesis in American History," Journal of American History 73 (June 1986): 120-136.

16.   Mary Beth Norton, Liberty's Daughters: The Revolutionary Experience of American Women, 1750-1800 (Boston: Little, Brown, 1980); Mari Jo Buhle, Women and American Socialism, 1870-1920 (Urbana: University of Illinois Press, 1981). For a more complete listing, see Elaine Tyler May, "Expanding the Past: Recent Scholarship on Women in Politics and Work," Reviews in American History 10 (December 1982): 216-233. Studies analyzing the intersection of work and race also appeared in the 1980s. See Lucie Cheng and Edna Bonavich, eds., Labor Immigration Under Capitalism: Asian Workers in the United States Before World War II (Berkeley and Los Angeles: University of California Press, 1984); Jacqueline Jones, Labor of Love, Labor of Sorrow (New York: Basic Books, Inc., 1985); Rosalinda M. Gonzalez "The Chicana in Southwest Labor History, 1900-1975 (A Preliminary Bibliographic Analysis)," Critical Perspectives of Third World America 2 (Fall 1984): 26-61.

17.   Christine Lunardini, From Equal Suffrage to Equal Rights: Alice Paul and the National Women's Party, 1913-1928 (New York: New York University Press, 1986). DuBois, Feminism and Suffrage.

18.   Buechler, The Transformation of the Woman Suffrage Movement; Felice Gordon, After Winning.

19.   Susan Reverby, "The Labor and Suffrage Movements: A View of Working-Class Women in the Twentieth Century," in Liberation Now (New York: Dell Publishing Co., 1971), 94-101; Meredith Tax, The Rising of the Women (New York: Monthly Review Press, 1980); Nancy Schrom Dye, As Equals and as Sisters (Columbia: University of Missouri Press, 1980); Diane Balser, Sisterhood and Solidarity (Boston: South End Press, 1987); DuBois, "Working Women, Class Relations, and Suffrage Militance," 34-58.

20.   Nancy F. Cott, The Grounding of Modern Feminism (New Haven: Yale University Press, 1987), 7.

21.   Tentler, Wage-Earning Women, 4, 26-80; Kennedy, If All We Did Was To Weep At Home, 112-131; Sarah Eisenstein, Give Us Bread But Give Us Roses (London: Routledge and Kegan Paul, 1983), 2-33.

22.   Lillian Matthews, Women in Trade Unions in San Francisco, University of California Publications in Economics, vol.3 (Berkeley: University of California Press, 1913), 92, 94.

23.   Daniel Rodgers, "In Search of Progressivism," <u>Reviews in American History</u> 10 (December 1982): 114. Rodger's article responded to Peter Filene's "An Obituary for 'The Progressive Movement'" which was the initial work to question whether progressivism in its totality could be regarded as one movement. It was Filene who called for a shift "away from convenient synthesis and toward multiplicity," preferring to characterize the period as one of "shifting coalitions around different issues." Peter G. Filene, "An Obituary for 'The Progressive Movement'," <u>American Quarterly</u> 22 (1970): 33. Nancy Cott observed that the periods of greatest activity in feminist movements "exhibit not 'unity' but strategic coalition" and "a spectrum of conceptualizations" on the role of women in society. Nancy F. Cott, "Feminist Theory and Feminist Movements" in <u>What Is Feminism?</u>, Juliet Mitchell and Ann Oakley, eds. (New York: Pantheon Books, 1986), 59.

24.   Kerber and De Hart-Mathews, <u>Women's America</u>, 224-225. In the book's introduction, Kerber and De Hart-Mathews acknowledge their debt to Joan Kelly with regard to their perspective on women in history. Kelly posited that "women's place is not a separate sphere or domain of existence but a position within social existence generally." When Kerber and De Hart-Mathews call for a refocusing, they ask us to see women in this light, acting in and interacting with all aspects of history and life. Joan Kelly, <u>Women, History and Theory</u> (Chicago: The University of Chicago Press, 1984), 57.

CHAPTER 1

"YES, WE ARE POLITICIANS":

SAN FRANCISCO WOMAN UNIONISTS AND FEMINISM, 1900-1911

> "Now when we want anything we go right to a politician and get
> it. . . .Yes, we are politicians. We go into politics."
>
> Louise LaRue, Secretary
> Waitresses' Union Local 48
> September 29, 1909

Until the 1970s, the middle and upper classes appeared to be the bastions
of American feminism, as theory and in its practice.   Historical and
contemporary explorations of feminism's participants, organizations, and
ideology seldom cited working-class women's involvement or acknowledged that
issues of class played a role in shaping feminism's goals and tenets.   Few
scholars examined working-class women in the context of either feminism or
political processes. This omission both reflected and perpetuated the assumption
that a feminist consciousness was not present among these women.   At best,
their presumed nonparticipation relegated them to the sidelines during periods of
feminist activism.

This perspective has given way to a rich debate in the last decade over
the role of class in the formation of feminist consciousness and whether a
"distinctive (working-class) variant of feminism" exists.   Maurine Weiner
Greenwald contributed to this discourse in her study of the divergent views

expressed by women in the labor press on whether married women should work outside the home in post-World War I Seattle. Greenwald contended that working-class feminism distinguished itself from the middle-class variety by its attempt to reconcile "their individual and collective aspirations as women with loyalties felt as members of the working class."[1]

Other scholars have emphasized that feminism, like other ideologies, flows from material conditions. In her study of modern Canadian working-class feminism, Heather Jon Maroney agreed that this branch of the women's movement "had its own outlook on what feminism should be." She asserted that this distinction existed because working-class feminism "was rooted in the workplace."[2]

Female leaders of the San Francisco labor movement formulated their own brand of feminism during the campaign for female enfranchisement in California. They founded a separate organization, the Wage Earners' Suffrage League (WESL) in September 1908 as a tangible expression of their commitment to the suffrage cause and their need for an autonomous structure to promote their vision of suffrage. The WESL was one of several such groups throughout the United States during the latter part of the suffrage movement.

At the turn of the century, San Francisco was an immigrant, Catholic town containing a sizable working-class population. Wage-earning women comprised a significant section of this community. A large number of San Francisco workers belonged to labor unions, including ten percent of all non-domestic female wage-earners. In the century's first decade, labor's voice exercised considerable influence in city hall. Mayor Eugene Schmitz and a growing number of city supervisors campaigned for and won elective office as candidates of the worker-backed Union Labor Party (ULP). Even the scandal of 1907 barely affected the party's fortunes; city voters put ULP candidate P.H. McCarthy, president of the Building Trades Council, in the mayor's seat in 1909. The ULP also dominated the Board of Supervisors and was the party in office in San Francisco during the 1911 California campaign for woman suffrage.[3]

The WESL rose out of these circumstances and conditions. Specifically, its members led those unions dominated by women; most significantly Waitresses' Local 48. While influenced by the rise of feminism among middle-class women, they derived their own convictions from their experiences as wage-earners and union activists.

ETHNICITY

In order to examine the factors which contributed to the development of feminist sentiments among San Francisco's female unionists, we must first survey the environment in which they lived. In crossing the threshold of her home on the way to work, the average San Francisco female wage-earner in 1910 stepped into a milieu shaped by the white ethnic character of the city's population. In contrast to the native midwestern and Protestant populace of Los Angeles at the turn of the century, San Francisco was an immigrant, Catholic town. While almost sixty-five percent of the city's residents in 1910 were born in the United States, 36.9 percent of these natives had foreign-born parents. Second-generation Americans were closely bound to their ethnic traditions and communities. Together with foreign-born residents, they comprised over two-thirds of San Francisco's population (See Table 1).[4] Most city residents were Catholic and Roman Catholic churches represented the largest number of houses of worship of any denomination in the city.[5]

By 1911, among those San Franciscans of foreign stock, the Irish clearly predominated; they represented almost one-fourth of second-generation residents. Germans ranked second, followed by a growing Italian community (see Table 2).[6]

TABLE 1

NATIVITY OF ALL SAN FRANCISCO RESIDENTS, 1910

Native-born of Native parents	115,359	(27.7%)
Native-born of Foreign parents	153,781	(36.9%)
Foreign Born	130,874	(31.4%)
Total	416,912	(100.0%)

Source: U.S. Bureau of the Census, Thirteenth Census of the United States: Abstract of the Census with Supplement for California, 616.

TABLE 2

SAN FRANCISCO FOREIGN-BORN WHITE STOCK, 1900 AND 1910

Germany	68,758	Ireland	66,784
Ireland	59,705	Germany	59,401
Great Britain	19,249	Italy	29,081
Italy	14,644	Scandinavia	20,602
Scandinavia	14,227	Great Britain	20,455
Other*	65,237	Other*	88,332
	241,820		284,655

*Includes those of mixed foreign parentage

Source: U.S. Bureau of the Census, Thirteenth Census, Vol. 1, Part 1: 949.

Members of these groups, particularly those of foreign stock in the working classes, tended to settle in certain areas of San Francisco. Irish and German working-class communities thrived in the Mission district, especially in the aftermath of the 1906 earthquake. Many Irish working-class families in the adjoining South-of-Market district drifted into the Mission when their homes succumbed to the earthquake and resultant fire. The Italian population, residing mainly in the North Beach and rural Portola areas, partially shifted into the Mission after the earthquake and fire destroyed substantial parts of North Beach. Until the second World War, the Mission remained "consciously Irish, often consciously working class," according to William Issel and Robert W. Cherny. The Mission of the early twentieth century could also be described as consciously Catholic.[7]

The demographics of wage-earning women in San Francisco in 1910 parallel those of the working class as a whole. Women constituted 43.2% of the total population and 18.4% of the city's labor force. Many female workers were white native-born women with foreign-born parents (43.6%). If these women are combined with their foreign-born counterparts, white female wage-earners of foreign stock constituted 71.3% of the total group, giving the San Francisco female labor force a heavily ethnic character (See table 3). Chinese, Black, Japanese and other women of color constituted only .68% of the general population and 1.7% of the female workforce.[8]

One-third of all employed women in San Francisco at the turn of the century were Irish. This represented the highest labor participation rate of any ethnic group, including native-born women, who exhibited a labor participation rate of 21.8%. Irish women included 37% of all servants and waitresses, 37% of all female laundry workers, 30% of all female teachers and 40% of all female laborers. These figures agree with studies by Barbara Klaczynska and Joan Dickinson showing that Irish women exhibited the highest labor participation rate of any ethnic group in the United States during this period.[9]

TABLE 3

NATIVITY OF SAN FRANCISCO WAGE-EARNING WOMEN, 1910

White Foreign-born	11,408	(27.7%)
White Native of Foreign Parentage	17,948	(43.6%)
White Native-born	11,090	(27.0%)
Black	260	(0.6%)
Native American, Chinese, Japanese and all other	444	(1.1%)
Total	41,150	

Source: U.S. Bureau of the Census, Thirteenth Census, 4: 601

In her study of Philadelphia female wage-earners in the early twentieth century, Klaczynska notes that Irish women had worked outside their homes prior to immigration, particularly in domestic service. Their higher rate of literacy and ability to speak English also made them more desirable workers. Also, as an older and more assimilated ethnic group, the Irish community found working an acceptable activity for women, necessary for mobility into the middle class. Finally, more single Irish women were arriving in the United States at this time; they needed to be able to support themselves. Hasia Diner commented that "the woman who had never worked rarely figured in the Irish-American social portrait."[10] Early San Francisco history documents the presence of Irish female wage earners. In the early 1870s, the California Labor Exchange reported that the demand for domestics was double the number of servants available. During the years 1868-1871, the Exchange placed 1402 women, more than one thousand Irish, in domestic positions. When San Francisco workingmen rose up against the presence of Asian laborers in San Francisco in the late 1870s, they claimed to protest, in part, on behalf of their sisters and daughters. Among the movement's accusations was the charge that Chinese cheap labor threatened the employment of these Irish female servants. "Our Women Are Degraded by Coolie Labor!" proclaimed one banner. Irish female wage-earners, then, appeared to be a significant feature of the San Francisco life before 1900.[11]

Despite the fact that Germans ranked highest numerically of all ethnic groups in San Francisco in 1900, German women constituted only 15% of all employed women. They mostly worked in white collar and mercantile occupations. Nationally, 12.4% of immigrant German women worked.[12]

Italian women showed the lowest labor participation rate of any ethnic group nationally. Because they had a low literacy rate and a lesser ability to speak English, they were less desirable as domestics and industrial workers. Italian women were also more apt to stay in their own neighborhoods, among their peers, and within their own families. Unlike Irish women, Klaczenska commented, the Italian community and family assigned women a role of specific obligations and duties which proved to be antithetical to obtaining wage work outside the home. Italian women represented only 2.3% of all documented wage-earning females in San Francisco in 1900 and tended to work in Italian-dominated fields of employment in North Beach. According to Lillian Matthews, Italian women comprised most of the newly organized union of cracker bakers and were beginning to enter the garment industry in significant numbers. Robert E.L. Knight and Glenna Matthews also documented the presence of Italian women in the canneries of the Bay Area (See Table 4).[13]

Irish women also involved themselves in organizational activity designed to benefit their community's less fortunate. In particular, Irish nuns committed their lives to serve their needy compatriots and directed much attention towards secular women. The Sisters of Mercy offered Mercy Houses for destitute, abused, and "fallen" women, training schools for women wanting to enter nursing or clerical work, employment agencies for domestics, and day care for the children of working mothers in San Francisco and other cities. Nuns administered these programs and provided direct services. In Irish communities, nuns' orders played a significant role within these institutions, particularly those geared to disadvantaged women. This communal model of gender-based social welfare surely served as a powerful example to Irish women. Some would carry this model of service and leadership into the world of wage work.[14]

TABLE 4

PARENTAGE OF SAN FRANCISCO WORKING WOMEN, 1900

Ireland	9196	(30.4%)
Germany	4526	(15.0%)
Great Britain	2117	(7.0%)
Scandinavia	1213	(4.0%)
Italy	693	(2.3%)
Other	5887	(19.5%)
Total of Foreign Parentage	23,632	(76.8%)
Native parentage	6593	(21.8%)
Total	30,225	(100%)

Source: U.S. Census Office, Twelfth Census, 20: 722-723

Ethnic culture filtered women's wage work experience in definite ways. As Barbara Klaczenska noted, "Women's ethnicity determined her image of herself as a worker and the community's approach to her employment."[15] Italian and Irish women viewed themselves very differently in terms of the meaning of wage work to their lives. Irish women essentially saw themselves as individuals with the potential for lifelong wage labor, if need be, and possessed "an economic sense of self."[16] The Italian community defined women's contribution to their families in non-economic terms, even if their function did bring an income to the household. Irish women, then, were the most numerically significant female wage earners in San Francisco during the early years of the twentieth century. Their primacy, however, extended beyond their demographic presence. Clearly, Irish women showed themselves to be the most visible, active and work-conscious element of San Francisco's female labor force during this period.

WAGE WORK
Demographics

According to commonly held assumptions, a domestic code for women enjoyed a hegemonic cultural dominance during the nineteenth century. This model of ladyhood which prescribed piety, purity, domesticity, and submissiveness for all females allegedly commanded unquestioning obedience or denunciation as a bluestocking or prostitute. The woman who remained in the home became the standard of respectability, a standard that wage-earning women found difficult to meet.[17]

However, recent studies question the cross-class assumptions of this view of women, postulating a more flexible relationship between women and work, especially in communities of immigrant and working-class people. Christine Stansell's examination of New York wage-earning women from 1789 until 1860 documents the presence of a family wage economy among the working poor.

Working women and children contributed a vital portion of the total family income needed to survive, and this necessity dictated an acceptance of laboring women in the community. Mary P. Ryan discovered that native-born, middle-class daughters, and sometimes mothers, in mid-century Utica worked so that the family's sons could prepare for professional and white-collar jobs. According to Hasia Diner, Irish immigrant women thought nothing of leaving home for domestic work in the nineteenth century because working out was a feature of their culture prior to emigration from Ireland. In her study of working women in Philadelphia, 1910-30, Barbara Klaczynska pointed out that while women usually worked out of need, necessity "was relative, reflecting their concept of life style, material possessions, and ambitions for their children."[18]

In his study of nineteenth-century workingmen in San Francisco, Jules Tygiel found, as had Stansell in New York, that each family member was considered a potential wage earner. Daughters were the most likely females of the family to enter the work force. As the century drew to a close, more families either sent children to work or admitted they did to census takers. Within this group, Tygiel showed that an increasing number of daughters secured gainful employment, rising from 35% of all daughters in the sample in 1880 to 50% in 1900. During that time period, the labor participation of women in San Francisco rose from 15.6% in 1880 to 18.4% in 1900 and 1910. The percentage of wage-earning women climbed from 21.6% to 26.8% of the total labor force in the same time span (Table 5).[19]

While the notion of women working had a certain amount of circumstantial acceptance in working-class communities throughout the 1800s, the idea of independent, self-supporting women did not attain this standing. The family wage economy persisted through the early twentieth century as dutiful daughters continued to turn their paychecks over to a parent.[20]

TABLE 5

SAN FRANCISCO WAGE-EARNING WOMEN, 1890-1910

	1890	1900	1910
Percentage of All Women Employed*	21.6%	23%	26.8%
Labor Participation Rate	15.6%	18.4%	18.4%

*Age 10 and older

Sources: U.S. Census Office, Eleventh Census, 1:728; Vol. 1, Part 1, 130; U.S. Census Office, Twelfth Census, Vol. 2, Part 2: 590; U.S. Bureau of the Census, Thirteenth Census, 4: 600-601; U.S. Bureau of the Census, Thirteenth Census of the United States: Abstract of the Census with Supplement for California, 593.

By the turn of the century, however, increasing numbers of middle-class women earned college degrees and became autonomous professionals. At the same time, growing numbers of wage-earning women left their families to seek work. While choice and a desire for freedom played a role, Joanne Meyerowitz identifies such factors as financial non-support from husbands and families, lack of jobs in their region, and family disintegration through death, desertion and divorce which added to the mass of women living apart from families and surviving on their own means.[21]

To make comparisons between national trends and the situation for San Francisco female wage-earners this study utilizes a database of San Francisco working women compiled by Ruth Shackelford at San Francisco State University. The database consists of 425 randomly selected women workers from the rolls of the 1900 United States Census.[22]

National estimates as to how many women lived on their own and supported themselves at this time range from ten to thirty percent. Women in the San Francisco sample fell at the high end of this continuum, with 31.8%

living apart from their families. Social agencies and reformers across the United States sometimes labeled these workers "women adrift." An additional 15.1% headed households and were responsible for dependents.(Table 6)[23]

Lyn Weiner indicates in her national study of wage-earning women that primarily younger women moved away from home in search of work in the United States during this period. Most of these adventurous women were in their teens, their numbers peaking at age 18, whereas their male counterparts tended to leave home in their early 20s. Analysis of the 1900 San Francisco sample, however, demonstrates that one-quarter of women living away from home in San Francisco were between the ages of twenty and twenty-seven with women between thirty-five and forty-nine constituting another one-fourth. Women in their teens, on the other hand, comprised only fifteen percent of the total number of women on their own. (Table 7)[24]

Weiner also observed that most women who lived away from home were foreign-born, comprising fifty percent of all boarders and lodgers. This figure, however, was influenced by the fact that many immigrant domestics lived with their employers. Weiner added, "When servants are excluded, native-born women become the first ranked group of boarders and lodgers." This apparently held true for San Francisco female wage-earners. While there is an almost equal split between immigrant and native-born women who lived away from home in the sample, accounting for domestics who boarded with their employers would cause natives to predominate in this category.(Table 8)[25]

Thus, while gainful employment for women had long played a role in working-class community life, autonomy and self support had become a new feature of this phenomenon. A significant number of San Francisco wage-earners lived apart from families or were primary breadwinners. As opposed to national figures, the bulk of these women were twenty and older. The largest single age group of "women adrift" was the thirty-to-forty-nine category.

TABLE 6

RESIDENTIAL STATUS OF SAN FRANCISCO
WAGE-EARNING WOMEN, 1900

Living with family	226	(53.2%)
Living apart	135	(31.8%)
Head of Household	64	(15.1%)
	425	(100%)

Source: Statistics generated from database compiled from 1900 United States Census manuscripts by Ruth Shackelford.

TABLE 7

AGES OF SF WAGE-EARNING WOMEN LIVING
APART FROM FAMILY, 1900

13 TO 19 YRS OLD	21	(10.6%)
20 TO 27 YRS OLD	49*	(24.6%)
28 TO 35 YRS OLD	35*	(17.6%)
36 TO 49 YRS OLD	55*	(27.6%)
50 YRS AND OLDER	38*	(19.1%)

*Includes women who were heads of households

Source: Statistics generated from 1900 San Francisco database

TABLE 8

NATIVITY OF SF FEMALE WAGE-EARNERS
LIVING AWAY FROM HOME, 1900*

IMMIGRANT	101	(50.8%)
NATIVE-BORN	98	(49.2%)
	199	

*Includes women who were heads of households

Source: Statistics generated from 1900 San Francisco database

The most critical factors determining the character of the white female labor force at this time were age and marital status. The bulk of women workers nationally, both native and foreign-born, were young and single. According to Leslie Tentler, 55% of women wage-earners in cities with populations over 100,000 were between 16 and 24 years of age prior to 1930. Tentler found that in 1908 75% of women factory workers and 63% of women in retail clerk occupations fell in this category with the largest number of women an adolescent 16 to 19 years old. Dickinson confirmed this was particularly true for foreign-born women.[26]

In the San Francisco sample, female wage-earners aged 16 to 20 years of age constituted the largest group ranked by age in the female work force (21.2%), yet almost 60% of the working women sampled were over age 24. The mean age of this group was almost thirty-one years. This suggests that San Francisco wage-earning women departed from national trends and worked until a later age. Census data suggests that this situation remained true for 1910 (See Table 9).[27]

One possible reason for this may have been due to the marital status of these women. At the turn of the century, the median marriage age for women in the United States was 22 years. However, in San Francisco, only 26.4% of women were wives by age 24, indicating that these women remained single longer than the national average. This seems unusual in a city where there were 135 men for every 100 women over fifteen. But most San Francisco men also waited until after age twenty-four to marry.[28]

TABLE 9

AGES OF SAN FRANCISCO WAGE-EARNING WOMEN, 1900

AGE GROUPS	ABSOLUTE FREQUENCY	RELATIVE FREQUENCY (PCT)	CUMULATIVE FREQUENCY (PCT)
40 TO 90 YRS	94	22.2	22.2
30 TO 39 YRS	89	20.9	43.1
25 TO 29 YRS	66	15.6	58.7
21 TO 24 YRS	68	16.0	74.7
16 TO 20 YRS	94	22.2	96.9
13 TO 15 YRS	13	3.1	100.0
MISSING CASES	1	.2	
TOTAL	425	100.0	

MODE: 16 TO 20 YRS

VALID CASES: 424   MISSING CASES: 1

Source: 1900 San Francisco Database

San Francisco's high proportion of Irish residents may account for these figures, particularly for women. In their homeland, Irish women lived in a sharply sex-segregated society where men and women led separate lives. Even though the family functioned as an economic unit, men and women ate, prayed, and socialized apart. If women did marry at all, they wed late in life. They carried this tendency with them when immigrating to the United States and continued to maintain this position through the second generation. Because of this tradition, self-support remained a concern for these women.[29]

Research on United States women between 1890-1920 has consistently shown that most women left the documented labor market after marriage, and returned only after an event or circumstance which severely lessened or eliminated the male wage-earner's income. According to Weiner, 76% of female wage earners in 1910 were single, divorced, or widowed. The labor force participation rate for married women was 11% compared to 48% for single women and 35% for widowed or divorced women. When wives did contribute to the family economy, it was a small amount, usually less than that of their daughter's. Dickinson discovered that while foreign-born wives were more apt to work for pay than native-born wives, marriage was the major deterrent to work outside the home, regardless of age or nativity. Working-class women fantasized that marriage would mean the end of employment outside the home for them, and that their husband's income would be enough to support a family. To work at home without pay was a sign of security and social respectability, while the need for outside employment signalled an economic crisis. A wife's income was "a working class family's final defence against destitution."[30]

The San Francisco sample reflects these findings. The three hundred single women account for over seventy percent of the Shackelford's sample. Widowed, divorced, and separated women, however, comprised almost one quarter of the total sample, a greater percentage than the twenty-eight working women who were married and living with their husbands (See Table 10).

Workers over twenty-one years of age and those who had been married at some point in their lives, then, comprised a significant part of the San Francisco female work force at the turn of the century.

The picture of San Francisco female wage-earners in the early twentieth century, then, was one of women older than the national average who remained single longer, with an extended history of self-support. The high percentage of Irish women wage-earners proved to be a contributing factor to this situation.

Occupations

One trend in employment persisted from the nineteenth century. The largest single occupational classification for San Francisco women in the 1910 Census remained servantry. Servants accounted for 15.1% of all working women. Domestic service was the most common occupation for women nationally until 1920, according to Lyn Weiner, employing more than twenty-five percent of American women. Dickinson also notes that servantry employed a high number of the foreign-born at this time. It was the bottom rung of the job ladder and, thus, the most accessible occupation to foreign-born workers, who were viewed as undesirable by many commercial and industrial employers.[31]

Servantry, however, declined as an occupational choice for women after the early 1900s. Because the 1900 census did not isolate the number of servants, but combined them with waitresses, it is not possible to demonstrate an exact rate of decline. Those numbers are available for 1910 and 1920, however, and in the course of that decade, female servants decreased to 13.6% of San Francisco wage-earning women.[32]

TABLE 10

MARITAL STATUS OF SAN FRANCISCO WAGE-EARNING WOMEN, 1990

MARITAL STATUS	ABSOLUTE FREQUENCY	RELATIVE FREQUENCY (PCT)
NEVER MARRIED	300	70.6
MARRIED	28	6.6
WIDOWED	73	17.2
DIVORCED	9	2.1
MARRIED BUT SEPARATED	15	3.5
TOTAL	425	100.0

MODE: NEVER MARRIED

VALID CASES: 425   MISSING CASES: 0

Source: 1900 San Francisco Database

Because of long hours, lack of privacy, poor pay, and arbitrary and cruel treatment by employers, second-generation women considered domestic service distasteful. Better assimilated and more literate than their parents, these women had the choice of the better-paying and more respectable clerical jobs in offices and industry. As a result, stenography/typewriter became the second largest occupation in 1910, employing 9.8% of San Francisco female wage earners. One half of these women were second-generation white women. By 1920, clerical occupations ranked highest for women and displaced many other traditionally female occupations such as servantry, the needle trades, or waitress work.[33]

Non-factory dressmakers and seamstresses comprised the third largest occupation, representing 9.0% of San Francisco working women in 1910. Nationally, needlework was the second most important category for women. Indeed, it was displacing domestic service as the occupation for the foreign-born in 1910. However, in San Francisco, commerce was the mainstay of the economy. While manufacturing was an important sector, only light industry had found a home there. Semi-skilled and unskilled jobs in industry were already dropping by 1880 while clerical work was on the rise (See Table 11).[34]

TABLE 11

MOST COMMON WOMEN'S OCCUPATIONS: SAN FRANCISCO 1910

Occupation	No. of Women Employed	Percent of Female Labor Force
Servants	6194	15.1%
Stenographer/ Typewriters	4032	9.8%
Dressmakers and Seamstresses	3712	9.0%
Saleswomen	2617	6.4%
Bookkeepers, cashiers and accountants	2360	5.7%
Teachers	1732	4.2%
Office clerks	1286	3.1%
Milliners and millinery dealers	1286	3.1%
Untrained midwives and nurses	1262	3.1%
Boarding and lodginghouse keepers	1247	3.0%
Trained nurses	1160	2.8%
Industrial laundresses	1120	2.7%
Waitress	977	2.4%
	28,982	70.5%

Source: U.S. Bureau of the Census, Thirteenth Census, 4:601

TABLE 12

WOMEN'S JOB CATEGORIES - SAN FRANCISCO 1910

Job Category	Number of Women	Percent of Female Labor Force
Clerical/ White Collar	16,263	39.5%
Domestic/ Personal Service	11,468	27.9%
Manufacturing/ Industrial	7806	19.0%
Other	618	1.5%
Undocumented	4995	12.1%
TOTAL	41,150	100 %

Source: U.S. Bureau of the Census, Thirteenth Census, 4:601

Indeed, the various clerical and white-collar occupations employed the greatest proportion of San Francisco women documented in the 1910 census. Almost forty percent of female wage-earners performed office work, clerked in wholesale and retail establishments, worked as telephone operators and practiced teaching or nursing. Those in domestic or personal service represented 24.8% of all working women. Aside from servantry, service workers were employed as waitresses, housekeepers, barbers and hairdressers, home laundresses, and untrained midwives and nurses. (See table 12)[35] Within personal service occupations, however, one was on the rise for female wage-earners. Waiting began as a male province and remained so throughout the nineteenth century. By 1900, however, women constituted forty percent of the occupation's practitioners nationally. Between 1900 and 1910, waitresses doubled their numbers and rose to forty-five percent of all of those waiting. Women dominated waiting in 1920, holding fifty-one percent of all waiting jobs. By this time, waiting ranked in the top twenty occupations for women in the United States.[36]

San Francisco displayed a trend not quite as strong, but nevertheless significant. While there are no separate figures for waitresses in 1900, the occupation ranked eleventh in 1910 as a job choice for San Francisco women. Women comprised twenty-four percent of all food servers. By 1920, women's relative numbers within the waiting craft, however, rose to almost thirty percent of all workers.[37]

Only 19% of San Francisco women were employed in manufacturing and industry. Included with non-factory dressmakers were milliners, industrial sewing operatives, industrial laundry workers, tailoresses, and women in printing and publishing. Women in the sewing trades represented 81.7% of all San Francisco women laboring in the manufacturing sector. Women's numbers in the industrial cluster of occupations showed an even more dramatic decrease than servantry. The number of women employed in these jobs fell seventeen percent in ten years.[38]

It is clear from the 1910 census data that women workers in San Francisco were segregated by sex into a small number of occupations. While San Francisco male workers labored in a wide number of industries, and a similar range of jobs within these industries, women were confined to those jobs that had been traditionally defined as female, such as domestic and sewing work, or occupations which had recently become feminized. Stenographers and typists in San Francisco were overwhelmingly female at this time. Women employed in clerical occupations which also included men were either in less-skilled positions or were paid at a wage at the lower end of the job's scale. This propensity in the San Francisco labor market reflected a national trend of occupational segregation by gender. Employer preferences, pressure from male workers and women's perception of themselves as potential wives and mothers rather than workers reinforced and perpetuated this segregation.[39]

One of the most striking features about San Francisco's female population in 1910 was the almost microscopic proportion of non-white women. Of a total of 180,011 women residing in the city, only 617 were Black (.3%) and 1347 were Chinese (.8%). Of the documented 260 black women employed in 1910, 65% were domestic servants with another 23.9% in other service jobs. Another 20 Blacks were non-industrial dressmakers. An extremely small number held industrial and white-collar jobs.[40]

The 1910 Census combined Chinese women with "Indians" and Japanese in its San Francisco table on occupations. It is therefore impossible to obtain an accurate count of working Chinese women or to determine where they worked from these figures. Most women in this category worked as servants or as nonindustrial seamstresses and dressmakers. In all likelihood, some businesses did not report their Chinese female workers to census surveyors. However, other sources indicate that many Chinese women worked in an occupation not documented in the published records - prostitution.[41]

Although these minute numbers of minority workers seem insignificant, the issue of race played a telling role for white female wage-earners, especially for those in labor unions. San Francisco unions protested as forcefully against the presence of nonwhite workers as they demanded union recognition and improved wages. By the late nineteenth and early twentieth century, most of their vehemence was directed against Asian labor. As we shall see, this reaction proved to be a critical element unifying the community of organized labor and had special implications for women.

It cannot be said that the sheer performance of wage work either liberates or politicizes individuals. Male wage workers in the early nineteenth century were considered less fit to vote because they relied on an employer for an income. Their lack of self-sufficiency, it was believed, made them vulnerable to influence and manipulation. Leslie Tentler concluded that women's work in the nineteenth and early twentieth century only served to preserve women's low status. Most work considered suitable for women paid low wages and frequently placed women in a powerless and subordinate position. For these women, wage labor paled next to visions of marriage and the relative control they could exert in the home.[42]

Wage work can be considered a wedge in the door between the private domestic sphere and public life. It allowed an opening wide enough for some women to glimpse the promise of greater citizenship with its privileges and advantages. Another factor was often needed to lead these women to a belief in enfranchisement and activity in its behalf, something which could challenge dominant assumptions about women and work, reinforce the positive aspects of wage-earning activities, and demonstrate the value of collective action for women. That factor was unionism.[43]

UNIONIZATION

San Francisco's vital and raucous atmosphere at the turn of the century spawned fictional heroines and heroes. Mary Condon, glovemaker and union president, sprang from Jack London's pen in his paean to pre-earthquake San Francisco working-class life, "South of the Slot." A rough-and-tumble rebel girl, Mary Condon displayed a toughness unfamiliar to ladies, when she demanded that a teamster show his union card. "No scab's going to handle that trunk. You ought to be ashamed of yourself, big coward, scabbing on honest men. Why don't you join the union and be a man?" she taunted the burly Bill Totts. Totts did produce a card, and later became Mary's "henchman and messenger" when she led a Laundry Workers' Union strike. At the story's climax, Mary engineered Bill's escape during a brawl between strikers and police. Whether at a Labor Council meeting or taking up the workers' cause, Mary's presence meant action.[44]

San Francisco labor history is full of women who could have inspired the creation of Mary Condon. The earliest example of working women organizing in San Francisco to improve their economic status appears to have been the Women's Cooperative Printing Union. Not a trade union, the WCPU was a print shop formed by women printers in 1868. After male union printers refused to work in any shop that employed women, Agnes Peterson applied to the National Typographical Union Local 21, San Francisco's printer union. "My request was treated with contempt," fumed Peterson. She and ten other women pooled their resources with six men to form the WCPU. Their venture survived until 1901.[45]

After emigrating from Ireland, Kate Kennedy worked as a San Francisco schoolteacher beginning in 1857 and rose to the position of principal by the 1870s. When she found her first paycheck to contain less than those received by men for the same job, Kennedy contested discriminatory pay for female teachers. She lobbied the state legislature, which passed a bill in 1874 granting equal pay to women in public school systems. The following year, Kennedy helped block an attempt to repeal the law and received a personal commendation from Susan B. Anthony and Elizabeth Cady Stanton for her efforts. An avowed single-taxer and member of the Knights of Labor by the 1880s, Kennedy also spoke publicly on behalf of woman suffrage, unionization, striking workers, and political reform. She died in 1890 shortly after winning a draining three-year battle in which she challenged her termination from the school system for political reasons.[46]

Effective union representation for women began in the 1880s. Typographical Union Local 21 allowed women members in 1883, after women printers operated presses during a strike. Lillian Matthews documented in her 1913 study of union women that the San Francisco's first female local was the Knights of Labor Ladies Assembly #5855. In February 1888, the Ladies' Assembly organized a mass meeting to discuss the plight of unorganized women and girls. Matthews commented that while organized labor expressed good intentions to change the situation, little resulted, except a call for women to organize on their own behalf. Not until 1891 did the first union primarily composed of women that survived into the twentieth century come into being. That year, female shoe factory workers formed the Boot and Shoe Fitters' Protective Union as an outgrowth of a successful strike over wages, hours, and working conditions. The San Francisco Council of Federated Trades recognized the women's union after a vigorous debate on whether women belonged on the Council.[47]

After 1900, women's organizing efforts proved to be more successful, partially due to the efforts of the San Francisco Labor Council. Formed in 1892 from the remnants of the Council of Federated Trades, the Council promoted the organization of such semi-skilled and unskilled workers as teamsters, laborers, waiters and waitresses, female laundry workers and factory production workers. Women, mostly employed in relatively unskilled jobs, benefited directly from this disposition. By 1913, fourteen unions with significant numbers of women had affiliated with the Labor Council. Although not all were prosperous locals, most female members expressed satisfaction with the unions and their impact on women's work lives (Table 13).[48]

For many Irish women and men in San Francisco, the labor movement insured self-respect and decent wages. Community leaders reinforced these positive effects of unionization. Father Peter Yorke, parish priest of a variety of churches with working-class congregations, espoused labor's cause at labor rallies, on picket lines and in his weekly paper, The Leader. He frequently used its pages as a soapbox from which to deliver orations in defense of the union movement and its members, whom he regarded as his flock.[49]

Because Irish women accounted for such a large percentage of San Francisco wage-earning women at the turn of the century, it is highly likely that they also predominated in the labor unions. Hasia Diner describes Irish women as being "extremely active" in the national trade union movement. Because a secure economic situation was a primary concern for these workers, they cared less about appearing unladylike or incurring public disapproval as union activists. Holding down such physically demanding jobs as laundresses and waitresses, where Irish women predominated, could only reinforce this inclination. Perhaps it also contributed to their determination to organize.

TABLE 13

SAN FRANCISCO FEMALE UNION MEMBERSHIP, 1913

Union	Membership
Steam Laundry Workers, Local No. 26	1100
Waitresses' Union Local 48*	536
United Garment Workers Local 131	500
Bindery Workers Local 125	275
Cracker Bakers' Auxiliary**	250
Journeymen Tailors No. 2	250
International Typographical Union No. 21	50
Musicians' Mutual Protective Union	50
Boot and Shoe Workers Union	39
Glove Workers' Union No. 39	35
Bottle Caners	32
Tobacco Workers Union	12
Office Employees Union	10
Press Feeders and Assistants	7
	3146

Source: Unless otherwise designated, Matthews, Women in Trade Unions in San Francisco, pp.10-85.

*Mixer and Server, (June 1911): 41; (July 1913): 46.
**Labor Clarion, 1 March 1912.

The Steam Laundry Workers Local #26 was one of the earliest unions to organize women in substantial numbers and it proved a great success story for San Francisco's female wage-earners.   Although predominantly a female industry, men working in the steam laundries initiated Local 26 in 1900. The union was organized along industrial lines and included all occupations housed in the laundries.   The men reluctantly allowed women into the local after an ultimatum from the international union. When the union hired laundress Hannah Mahoney Nolan as an organizer in 1901 women joined the local in large numbers.   After a sixteen-week campaign, the majority of male and female employees in San Francisco white steam laundries demanded and won union recognition.[50]

Prior to the contract, many women boarded at the laundry and were paid eight to ten dollars a month. Employees living at home received ten to twenty-five dollars a month but the wages of most did not exceed $17.50 per month. In reporting this, Matthews stressed that many employees were women with children. According to Nolan, laundry employees worked a seven-day week, from six A.M. until midnight each day.[51]

The April 1901 contract eliminated the boarding system and increased women's wages to six to ten dollars a week. The women worked a ten-hour day. They received time-and-a-half for overtime and an hour for lunch. The union fined workers who did not take their lunch break. In 1903, union members demanded and won the nine-hour day.[52]

By 1906, membership had grown to 1700 men and women, employed in 29 steam laundries. Most members found themselves homeless and jobless after the 1906 earthquake.   However, the union reorganized after the disaster, provided relief for members, and obtained jobs for 900 members in the nine laundries still standing. After its 1907 strike, the union, now stabilized at 1100 members, signed an agreement for a fifty-one hour week. The contract also provided for a yearly reduction in hours that culminated in the eight-hour day by

1910. By 1911, more than 60% of the women in the steam laundries were paid at least nine dollars a week or more, with most receiving nine to fifteen dollars a week. All white steam laundries in San Francisco were closed shops by 1910.[53]

Local 26 boasted that it had members of all ages and nationalities, and prided itself on having "many mature women" as members. These older women frequently worked in the higher-skilled areas of the laundries, according to Matthews. Despite this upbeat report, few women rose to leadership in Local 26 during this period. A smattering of women ran for union office in 1907 and in succeeding years. Secretary Carrie Parmer continued to hold her position through 1913, but most of the union's elected officials were men. Although women members of Local 26 outnumbered men five-to-one, men controlled the union. Lillian Matthews claimed that union leaders outside the local hoped Local #26 would split into separate female and male unions to eliminate friction between the sexes.[54]

The Waitresses' Union, Local 48, on the other hand, demonstrated that women could take charge of their own union affairs. Local 48 was initially a branch of the Cooks' and Waiters' Alliance. In April 1901, the almost 300 female members of the local joined their union brothers in a strike against San Francisco restaurants, demanding that the workday be decreased from fourteen to ten hours a day, that their wages be increased from four to five dollars a week to eight dollars, that they be paid an overtime rate of $.25 per hour, and that employers recognize the union. However, like many others that year, the strike failed and those members who had not been blacklisted returned to work under the old conditions.[55]

The Waitresses Union built up its membership over five years. By early 1906, the union won shorter hours, more sanitary kitchens, one-half hour for meals and one day off per week. The union scale provided a wage of $8-10 per week, depending on the number of straight hours worked and the amount of night work performed. A key part of the agreement was the provision detailing the work waitresses would not do including "shell peas, peel apples, . . . clean coffee urns, windows or ice boxes or scrub chairs." Union waitresses, exhibiting a firm craft identity, refused to perform work unconnected with customer service and negotiated agreements that included these stipulations in their contract.[56]

The Waitresses separated from Waiters Local 30 to start their own union, Local #48, in February 1906. In splitting off from the waiters, Local 48 followed suit with other waitresses' unions across the United States in forming sex-segregated culinary locals. Seventeen of these unions existed nationally by World War I. Waiters' Union official William Jefferson explained to readers of Mixer and Server, a culinary workers' journal, that "the girls thought it would be better to have a local of their own" because the women had separate goals and concerns. Local 30 leaders submitted the proposal to a vote and the membership granted the waitresses' request. Local 48 began with 250 members and survived the earthquake and fire several months later.[57]

By 1911, the union coffers paid three full-time officials--a secretary and two business agents. Other elected officers were paid $1-2 a month, depending on their duties. Paid officials were a luxury other San Francisco women's unions could not afford. The union averaged a membership of 536 waitresses in 1911, slightly more than half the number of documented women working in the trade.[58]

Dorothy Sue Cobble found that ethnic homogeneity characterized waitresses' locals in this period, especially in the West. Most of these women were native-born white women of Northern European descent, which would fit the profile of Irish predomination in San Francisco. This factor provided an element of cohesiveness among these women. In addition, Cobble noted that waitresses tended to live in nontraditional family settings as divorced, widowed, separated, or single women "adrift" and were more likely than women in other occupations to be primary wage earners. Louise LaRue, a Local 48 leader from its founding, was a widow. These characteristics combined with the camaraderie of teamwork on the jobs to create an environment of community and commitment within union locals.[59]

In contrast with the Steam Laundry Workers' Union, then, Waitresses' Local 48 separated from its parent union when its members recognized that their interests differed from those of the waiters. They established a successful local that continued to grow in numbers and developed a tier of leaders from its ranks that exercised control over the autonomous local. Other San Francisco female unions made comparable strides. In her study of California labor legislation prior to 1910, Lucile Eaves claimed that female union members in California demonstrated little interest in union affairs. Matthews' study, however, states that of all fourteen San Francisco unions with women members, half had female memberships active in union affairs and leadership ascended from the rank and file.[60]

While San Francisco working women may have been similar in many ways to their sisters nationally, one characteristic made them unique -- their opportunity to unionize. While no precise membership figures or percentages exist for San Francisco union women in this period, estimates based on reports to economist Lillian Matthews and figures reported in the labor press show that slightly over three thousand women were union members at this time. This roughly represented ten percent of all female wage-earners on the job outside of domestic service (See tables 12 and 13).[61]

Union figures for women nationally paled by comparison. In 1900, 3.3% of women in industrial jobs were organized onto unions. By 1910, that percentage dropped to 1.5%. Shortly afterward, a surge in garment industry organization brought many new women into the labor movement, and by 1920, 6.6% of wage-earning women were union members.[62]

The relatively high number of union women were probably due to several factors. First, San Francisco's unions represented 55,000 to 60,000 wage-earners at this time. Most unions were affiliated with the San Francisco Labor

Council. The total rank-and-file membership of the Labor Council unions was 40,000. Many unions, especially those in the powerful Building Trades Council were able to demand the closed shop and the eight-hour day. San Francisco was known as a union town in the first two decades of the twentieth century. Labor's strength and vitality inspired San Francisco working women to organize in greater numbers than in many other cities. Total union membership tripled between 1900 and 1915 in San Francisco.[63]

In addition, labor also had control over city government for all but two years between 1901 and 1911. The Union Labor Party was forged out of a waterfront strike in 1901 in which city police were used to protect strikebreakers. Irate unionists, determined that this would not happen again, formed the Union Labor Party (ULP). During the following decade, ULP candidates occupied the mayor's chair in four administrations out of five. P.H. McCarthy, president of the Building Trades Council was San Francisco's mayor in 1909-11, and the ULP held eleven out of eighteen seats on the Board of Supervisors at that time. The ULP's presence ensured a prolabor climate and, indeed, many labor disputes were settled in favor of labor during the ULP's reign. In his study of the Union Labor Party, Jules Tygiel concluded that the ULP was "a labor party in substance as well as in name" because workers voted it into power and because they believed that the ULP represented them. This atmosphere certainly produced an impact on women who sought to unionize.[64]

Labor unity in San Francisco, however, was not just a product of class solidarity. Labor scholars agree that one final element provided the glue for the labor community's cohesiveness: anti-Asian racism and an on-going campaign for Asian exclusion from the labor market. "The Chinese must go!" was the rallying cry of the Workingmen's Party in the late 1870s. The union label originated in San Francisco as a way to identify goods made by white workers, particularly clothing, shoes, and cigars. Labor strongly supported the federal Chinese Exclusion Act of 1882, which barred all but a few Chinese from immigrating to the United States, and the San Francisco Labor Council opposed the annexation of Hawaii and the Philippines, fearing a new flood of Asian unskilled workers. Organized labor formed or participated in a chain of clubs to stoke the flames of anti-Asian sentiment, including the League of Deliverance in 1882, the Asian Exclusion League in 1905, and the Anti-Jap Laundry League in 1908. Economist Lucile Eaves editorialized in 1910, "On the trade unionist of San Francisco has rested the responsibility for the campaign to exclude Oriental labor. . . This long campaign in front of what was felt to be a common enemy has contributed more that any other one factor to the strength of the California labor movement."[65]

Union women participated energetically in the movement to drive out Asian workers and business establishments. Waitresses' Union official Minnie Andrews represented the San Francisco Labor Council at Asiatic Exclusion League meetings, as did Labor Council delegate Rose Myears of Bindery Women Local 125. In 1909, Waitresses' Local 48 secretary Louise LaRue traveled to the National Women's Trade Union League convention in Chicago. During the plenary, she offered a resolution calling for the NWTUL's endorsement of federal exclusion laws against all Asians. LaRue alleged that Japanese men molested white children and willingly lived in filthy, crowded hovels as well as providing cheap labor that underbid that of whites. During the lengthy discussion on the resolution, LaRue testified that the resolution arose in the Laundry Workers Union and was officially sponsored by the San Francisco Labor Council. The convention defeated the measure, much to LaRue's dismay.[66]

Individual female unions in San Francisco forthrightly excluded women of color from their membership. Matthews reported that "all white women who are working at the craft are eligible for membership" in Local 48. A surviving union contract for the Waitresses' Union stipulated that "white women only" qualified for membership. The Steam Laundry Workers Union organized only those workers laboring in the white steam laundries and participated in the Anti-Jap Laundry League, a group founded by white laundry owners.[67]

This evidence substantiates Nancy Breen's conclusion that female unionism in San Francisco originated with women wage-earners' participation in the anti-Chinese and anti-Japanese movements of the late nineteenth and early twentieth century. When the Asian Exclusion Act of 1882 took effect, white women moved into the light industrial jobs formerly held by Chinese men. Initially encouraged to establish and associate with anti-Asian clubs by their employers at the turn of the century, these women may have developed the organizing and leadership skills which they brought to the union movement in these clubs. The anti-Asian movement provided San Francisco white women with an entree into the trade union establishment, while ongoing anti-Chinese and anti-Japanese activity of female unionists served to reinforce their solidarity with the white male union membership of the San Francisco Labor Council. San Francisco union women, then, contributed vigorously to the labor movement's anti-Asian campaign, sharing in labor's dark side as well as its accomplishments.[68]

The San Francisco labor press generally appeared to support the unionization of women during this period. As early as 1899, the Coast Seamen's Journal, the organ of the Sailors' Union of the Pacific, urged "all women who work for wages, of whatever occupation, to join in or form trade unions of their respective crafts." The Journal's coverage of women from 1908-13 was positive overall. It included many newsy items about union women in regular columns as well as separate articles and ran excerpts of Lillian Matthews's study of San Francisco union women. The Journal's motivation however, was not purely altruistic. Women should organize, the editors believed, to eliminate "female competition . . . thereby removing the employers' chance of making them undercut the wages established by the men." This level of coverage was astonishing in light of the fact that the SUP had, in all likelihood, no female members and few connections with women.[69]

The San Francisco Labor Council's paper, the Labor Clarion, also wrote generously on women and applauded their efforts to unionize, calling unions "the salvation of the woman worker." It ran a column on and for women from 1908 until 1911 which included a sprinkling of household hints but focused mainly on political and union news. Minna O'Donnell, an officer of the Women's Auxiliary of Typographical Union Local 21, authored the first few columns but most ran without a byline. The Clarion constantly referred to both men and women when addressing the labor community at large.[70]

In contrast, Organized Labor, the journal of the all-male Buildings Trades Council, carried little material of interest to or on behalf of women. Mainly, it offered an irregular column that contained romance fiction and home-making tips. A regular column which took union men to task for neglecting their families and urged the formation of women's auxiliaries ceased in 1903 after a three-year run. Organized Labor published little on women and unions, but did favor organization in preference to a legislated minimum wage.[71]

Michael Kazin reported in "Barons of Labor", a history of the San Francisco Building Trades Council, that buildings trades locals had an informal rule barring women from membership. Because the building trades were a closed-shop industry at this time, this effectively eliminated women from construction jobs. Indeed Kazin found that only 16 women worked in the skilled jobs in the building trades with another 43 as unskilled laborers.[72]

Reports published by professional women interested in union women's progress also revealed tensions between women and men in the broader labor movement. A secretary at "Labor Headquarters" confided to sociologist Jessica Peixotto in 1908 that "most men in the movement are either careless as to organizing women or else are opposed to it." Lillian Matthews's landmark 1913 work on San Francisco trade union women contained accounts of strained relations between men and women within unions. Two years after female cloakmakers joined the United Garment Workers Local 131, male cutters resented that female sewers spoke up for their own demands, rather than rely on the men to represent them. The cutters withdrew from the union and formed their own local. When this failed, the women refused to re-admit them into Local 131. While the male and female bindery locals generally enjoyed a friendly relationship, jurisdictional disputes sometimes arose when the men believed that certain work assigned to the women should fall to them. The two groups haggled for two years over whether men or women should operate folding machines.[73]

By 1920, Louise Ploeger still complained, "Both union men and employers have done much to keep women from becoming organized." She commented that when men did recognize that women should organize, it was still out of self-interest and a desire to eliminate competition for jobs.[74]

This period witnessed the formation and development of two separate women's union locals. Whether it was because of the tension described above, a need for autonomy due to a divergence in group interests or some other factor, two women's unions split away from their parent organizations. As discussed, Waitresses' Local 48 separated itself from Waiters' Local 30 in 1906 and the Cracker Bakers Auxiliary maintained itself as a local distinct from the Cracker Bakers beginning in 1911. In doing so, they joined ranks with the only female local in San Francisco, the Bindery Women's Union Local 125, founded in 1902 with the aid of the male Bookbinder's Union. These three locals represented almost one-third of all unionized women in San Francisco in 1913. Women also organized labor groups that brought together female unionists from several locals as well as the relatives of male unionists. The first such group was the Women's International Union Label League, formed in 1905 to promote the purchase of union-made goods by men and women in organized labor. The San Francisco

Labor Council recognized the group and listed it in its roster of official labor organizations.[75]

THE WOMAN MOVEMENT AND SUFFRAGE

While union activity pushed wage-earning women toward greater assertiveness and autonomy and enabled them to see themselves as active members of a community, the most obvious influence on all women with regard to suffrage was the feminist movement itself. From the start, demands for the "social, civil and religious rights of women" sparked the participation of wage-earning women. Nineteen-year-old Charlotte Woodward, an upstate-New York farmer's daughter who performed piecework at home for a nearby glove factory, enlisted several friends to join with her in attending the Seneca Falls Woman's Rights Convention in 1848. Woodward was the only surviving signer of the convention's Declaration of Sentiments to vote following the passage of the Nineteenth Amendment in 1920.[76]

Elizabeth Cady Stanton, Seneca Falls' main organizer and a key theorist and leader of the feminist movement until the 1890s, founded the Working Women's Association (WWA) in 1868 with Susan B. Anthony, another guiding light of nineteenth-century feminism. Stanton and Anthony proposed the WWA in order to promote the notion that suffrage was the primary tool for the betterment of working women. However, such WWA members as compositor Augusta Lewis expressed more concern over more practical and immediate matters such as wages, hours, and working conditions. Lewis held that union organizing promised more concrete gains for herself and her sisters and indeed responded to the International Typographical Union's (ITU) unwillingness to unionize women by forming Women's Typographical Union No.1 in New York City later in 1868. These tensions haunted the WWA throughout its brief existence and were responsible for its demise in late 1869 when Anthony's support of strike-breakers during a printer's strike only confirmed the unionists' distrust of middle-class women and their tactics. Just as Anthony and Stanton had little faith in unionization without the ballot, working women like Lewis saw suffrage as merely a pie-in-the-sky panacea.[77]

After this, suffragists made little attempt to join in coalition with working-class women; wage-earners preferred to commit their energy to struggles in their own community rather than grapple with an abstract notion of sex equality. For instance, an estimated 50,000 women joined the Knights of Labor during the 1880s, comprising one-tenth of its membership.[78]

Middle-class women, however, did not lose interest in their laboring sisters. They took a particular interest in "women adrift." Middling women attempted to take these "girls" under their wing through the formation of benevolent societies such as the Young Women's Christian Association and the Women's Educational and Industrial Union. While providing working women with reading rooms, lunch rooms, and some housing, these well-meaning organizations also tried to mold wage-earning women to conform with their definition of respectability. Women's hotels run by these groups imposed strict rules of behavior; social workers advised working women to choose "occupations which would enable women to utilize their special moral qualities." In other words, the WEIU promoted domestic jobs over less womanly factory work. California's WEIU formed a protective society to aid San Francisco working women in need but gained a reputation as a school for training women to be servants; thereby failing to attract those it sought to serve. The San Francisco WEIU's roster of officers included suffragists such as Selina Solomon, Mary Sperry and Ellen Clark Sargent.[79]

The late 1890s and early 1900s brought organizations that were of more use to female wage-earners, although their approach continued to be maternal. The National Consumer's League's (NCL) purpose was to identify those employers who allowed women to toil in unsanitary conditions and to initiate boycotts against them. The group issued labels to employers it considered satisfactory. While this was a more positive action by middle-class ladies, these benefactresses had no intention of empowering working-class women to act on their own behalf. Rather, they expected their wage-earning sisters to defer to their opinion and guidance, and to look up to them as daughters to their mothers. The NCL rarely supported women's labor strikes. Many NCL members were also suffragists.[80]

Meanwhile, in the latter part of the nineteenth century, working women continued to organize on their own behalf without the assistance of women in the more leisured classes. Female wage-earners organized themselves into unions of shoe workers, collar launderers, and textile mill workers. In addition, women joined male unions such as the National Union of Cigar Makers and the International Typographical Union, which officially opened its doors to women in 1878.[81]

By the turn of the century, national women labor leaders realized they could expect little more than half-hearted support from their male counterparts, much less aid in the form of female organizers and direct financial assistance. In 1903, they attempted, as they had over thirty years before, to combine with middle-class women in an organization based on gender unity and a desire to improve working conditions for women. This time, however, the group recognized and approved of union formation as a primary goal. Suffrage became an important but secondary purpose. The National Women's Trade Union League (NWTUL) was the culmination of the cooperative work between middle-class and working-class women in the settlement house movement.[82]

Dissatisfied with the incomplete results produced by the National Consumer's League, working women and their middle-class allies formed a body defined by historian Robin Jacoby as "the woman's branch of the labor movement and the industrial branch of the women's movement." Professional women, settlement workers, society wives, and suffragists worked with laboring women, not for them. According to historian Ellen Carol DuBois, the NWTUL provided "an arena to articulate working-class feminism related to, but distinct from, that of elite women." [83]

As well-intentioned and inspired as this concept was, in practice the group failed to weld unionism and feminism together successfully. In her history of the New York chapter, Nancy Schrom Dye revealed that the NWTUL was not truly cross-class in nature as the middle class and wealthy women dominated policy-making bodies for most of its existence. Class-based disagreement and rancor characterized the group's internal functioning. Pauline Newman, an organizer for the International Ladies' Garment Workers Union, commented that by 1914, the New York NWTUL consisted of two camps, "social workers and trade unionists." She and Rose Schneiderman, a leader of the Cap Makers' Union, briefly left the organization in disillusionment. That year, the NWTUL's primary focus shifted from unionization to protective legislation and suffrage. By World War I, the NWTUL completed the transition to a social welfare organization and most of the members committed to unionization left the organization. [84]

Few NWTUL chapters formed west of St. Louis, due to a dearth of middle-class sympathizers. [85] San Francisco wage-earning women, however, were on the move in their own behalf. Wage-earning women had begun to function politically, even before they organized themselves into unions. Women laundry workers, for instance, lobbied for an ordinance in 1900 limiting the workday in steam laundries to thirteen hours just prior to the formation of their union. [86]

With unionization, political efforts of female wage-earners gained greater coordination and structure. The Waitresses' Local 48 used a non-discrimination clause in the California constitution in 1906 to argue successfully that women should not be barred from working in establishments which served liquor. Lillian Matthews reported that the Waitresses Union "mix[ed] in municipal politics." [87]

Louise LaRue, Local 48's secretary, confirmed that. "Now, when we want anything, we go right to a politician and get it. We have everything we want," she boasted at the 1909 NWTUL convention in Chicago. "Yes, we are politicians. We go into politics." LaRue added that the local had campaigned for Union Labor Party mayoral candidate P. H. McCarthy in 1907 and would campaign again that fall.[88]

In 1907, LaRue and other women unionists joined forces with reform suffragists in the struggle for female enfranchisement. This alliance faced a road as rocky as the New York NWTUL but the trip would be much shorter. Unionists eventually formed their own suffrage organization in 1908, the San Francisco Wage Earners' Suffrage League, in order to carry on the effort in the labor community.

San Francisco women had performed wage labor in growing numbers since the nineteenth century. By the early twentieth century, they formed a significant part of the local labor force. As with their national counterparts, these women moved out of domestic service and industrial jobs in increasing numbers and into occupations such as clerical work and waitressing, which employed a growing number of women. Irish women emerged as a pivotal segment of the female labor force because of their Northern European heritage, their ability to speak English and their cultural expectation of long-term self-support. For these women especially, waitressing increasingly became a means of earning wages for themselves and their families.

By 1910, women comprised a significant and committed segment of the San Francisco organized labor community. They participated in locals with men, served on the San Francisco Labor Council and were active in movements deemed vital to labor, such as the drive to exclude Asians from the work force. They also formed autonomous locals and labor organizations which pursued goals supported by the labor community as a whole as well as addressing issues specific to wage-earning women. The Waitresses' Union Local 48 was the largest of these independent female locals.

Dorothy Sue Cobble found that the food service unions' structure promoted a high level of activity and leadership among unionized waitresses. The unions mixed an industrial design for the international organization, admitting workers from all branches of the trade and thereby facilitating women's entry into the union, with a local craft structure. The craft local encouraged "pride in the trade and loyalty to others who belonged to the same occupation," as it reinforced and institutionalized a distinct waitresses' work culture. It also provided women with a space apart from the predominantly male union culture, one that could be antagonistic to women and their involvement in the union. The fact that many waitresses functioned as primary wage earners contributed to this situation.   Those of us concerned with the history of female unionism must therefore take structure into account when investigating the varying receptivity of unions to women and the mechanisms which encouraged female autonomy and leadership.[89]

According to Nancy Cott's definition of modern feminism, women unionists instrumental in forming autonomous women's locals, especially those in Waitresses' Local 48, fit the bill. Cott identified three core components that denote twentieth-century feminism: the perception of gender-group identity, opposition to a gender-based hierarchy, and the recognition of the potential for change due to the fact that conditions are socially constructed and not divinely or naturally ordained. I would add that class as well as gender defined their self-perception and the institutions they would create. Through the founding of locals separate from those of union men performing the same craft, these female unionists affirmed their distinct gender-based identity. They expressed their opposition to sex hierarchy in their objections to a male leadership setting their agenda and acting on their behalf. As female unionists, they were also cognizant of their ability to improve their situation (and that of their membership) as workers and as women. Their willingness to designate themselves as "politicians" demonstrated their interest and their attraction to political processes and solutions. Through their actions and beliefs, these women exemplified a working-class variant of feminism that would carry them into the suffrage movement and the leadership of the WESL.[90]

Gender consciousness, activism, desire for participation in political processes, and training for leadership began on their own shop floors and in their locals, and would be easily transferred to the cause for suffrage. Because their feminism sprang from different roots, union suffragists brought very different values and beliefs to the suffrage movement. These differences would flavor the interactions between them and their middle-class counterparts throughout the campaign for woman suffrage in California.

NOTES TO CHAPTER ONE

1.   Maurine Weiner Greenwald, "Working-Class Feminism and the Family Wage Ideal: The Seattle Debate on Married Women's Right to Work" Journal of American History 76 (June 1989): 119,121. I am indebted to Professor Greenwald. Her paper helped guide me in shaping this chapter conceptually.

2.   Heather Jon Maroney, "Feminism At Work," in What Is Feminism?, ed. Juliet Mitchell and Ann Oakley (New York: Pantheon Books, 1986), 104.

3.   The San Francisco Board of Supervisors was, and continues to be, the combined city council and county board in the city's consolidated government.

4.   U.S. Bureau of the Census, Department of Commerce and Labor, Thirteenth Census of the United States: Abstract of the Census with Supplement for California (Washington, D.C.: Government Printing Office, 1913), 616.

5.   U.S. Bureau of the Census, Department of Commerce, Religious Bodies, 1916, Part I (Washington, D.C.: Government Printing Office, 1919), 330, 351, 490. Robert W. Cherny cautions that using data from the census reports on religious bodies is problematic as the methods different bodies used to count their membership varied. While Catholics included all those baptized as members, Protestants counted those eligible for communion and Jewish figures contained only heads of households. Cherny's estimates based on the census figures, however, demonstrate that more than half of all church-goers in 1890 were Catholic. Robert W. Cherny, "Pattern of Toleration and Discrimination in San Francisco," paper delivered at the annual meeting of the California American Studies Association, Long Beach, April 24, 1986.

6.   U.S. Bureau of Census, Department of Commerce and Labor, Thirteenth Census of the United States: 1910, 11 vols. (Washington, D.C., 1914), Vol. 1, Part 1, 949.

7.   William Issel and Robert W. Cherny, San Francisco, 1865-1932 (Berkeley and Los Angeles: University of California Press, 1986), 63-66.

8.   U.S. Bureau of Census, Thirteenth Census of the United States: Abstract with Supplement of California, 616; U.S. Bureau of Census, Thirteenth Census of the United States: 1910, 4: 600-601; U.S. Bureau of Census, Thirteenth Census of the United States: Abstract with Supplement of California, 593.

9.   U.S. Census Office, Department of the Interior, Twelfth Census of the United States: 1900, 37 vols. (Washington ,D.C.: Government Printing Office, 1902-1904), 20: 720-24.   Barbara Klaczynska, "Why Women Work: a Comparison of Various Groups - Philadelphia, 1910-1930," Labor History 17 (Winter 1977): 81; Joan Dickinson, The Role of Immigrant Women in the U.S. Labor Force, 1890-1910 (New York: Arno Press, 1980), 68-69.   Unlike the 1900 data, census tables for 1910 do not provide a breakdown of wage-earning women by their parent's nativity.

10.   Klaczynska, "Why Women Work," 81-82; Dickinson, Role of Immigrant Women, 89-90; Hasia Diner, Erin's Daughters in America, (Baltimore: Johns Hopkins University Press, 1983), 74.

11.   Lucile Eaves, A History of California Labor Legislation with an Introductory Sketch of the San Francisco Labor Movement, University of California Publications in Economics, vol. 2 (Berkeley: University of California Press, 1910), 311.

12.   Issel and Cherny, San Francisco, 1865-1932, 58; Dickinson, Role of Immigrant Women , 89.

13.   Klaczynska, "Why Women Work", 77-79; Dickinson, Role of Immigrant Women,   93, Lillian Matthews, Women in the Trade Unions in San Francisco, University of California Publications in Economics, vol. 3 (Berkeley: University of California Press, 1913), 63, 71; Robert Edward Lee Knight, Industrial Relations in the San Francisco Bay Area, 1900-1918, (Berkeley and Los Angeles: University of California Press, 1960), 276; Glenna Matthews, "The Fruit Workers of the Santa Clara Valley: Alternative Paths to Union Organization During the 1930s," Pacific Historical Review 54 (February 1985): 53-54.

14.   Diner, Erin's Daughters in America, 129-134. The Italian community also had its share of benevolent associations to care for the community's needy members. Few seemed to be directed at or run by women. On the other hand, Klaczenska and Yans-McLaughlin intimated that Italian women provided services to the community in their homes, such as housing and feeding boarders. Dino Cinel, From Italy to San Francisco: The Immigrant Experience (Stanford: Stanford University Press, 1982), 200-205; Deanna Paoli Gumina, Italians of San Francisco, 1850-1930 (New York: Center for Migration Studies, 1978),161-169, 177-8; Klaczenska, "Why Women Work," 74; Virginia Yans-McLaughlin, "Italian Women and Work: Experience and Perception," in Milton Cantor and Bruce Laurie, ed., Class, Sex and the Woman Worker (Westport, Conn.: Greenwood Press, 1979), 107-109.

15.   Klaczenska, "Why Women Work," 87.

16.   Diner, Erin's Daughters in America, 103.

17.   Alice Kessler-Harris, Out To Work (New York and Oxford: Oxford University Press, 1982), 49-56. For the classic article on the domestic code, see Barbara Welter, "The Cult of True Womanhood: 1820-1860," American Quarterly 18 (Summer 1966): 151-174.

18.   Christine Stansell, City of Women (New York: Alfred A. Knopf, 1986), 52-54, 105-129; Mary Ryan, The Cradle of the Middle Class (Cambridge: Cambridge University Press, 1983), 165-179; Diner, Erin's Daughters in America, pp. 70-105; Barbara Klaczynska, "Why Women Work", 73-87. Current studies also stress that women may have been undercounted when work was documented, and that perceptions of work by both women and men affect how it is reported. Dickinson, Role of Immigrant Women, 24; Virginia Yans-McLaughlin, "Italian Women and Work," 101-116.

19.   Jules Tygiel, "Workingmen in San Francisco, 1880-1901" (Ph.D dissertation: University of California, Los Angeles, 1977), 215-220.

20.   Kessler-Harris, Out To Work, 126-127; Leslie Tentler, Wage-Earning Women: Industrial Women and Family Life in the United States 1890-1910 (New York: Arno Press, 1980), 85-114.

21.   Lynn Weiner, From Working Girl to Working Mother (Chapel Hill: University of North Carolina Press, 1985), 24-25; Joanne Meyerowitz, Women Adrift: Independent Wage Earners in Chicago, 1880-1930 (Chicago: University of Chicago Press, 1988), 1-2. For an excellent portrayal of the community of single working women in New York in the years prior to the Civil War, see Christine Stansell, City of Women. See also Meyerowitz, Women Adrift for another local study. The classic study on single female wage earners was conducted by Congress at the urging of reformers Jane Addams and Florence Kelley and was part of a nineteen-volume series documenting the status of women workers at the turn of the century-U.S. Congress, Women Adrift, Volume 5 in Report on the Condition of Woman and Child Wage Earners in the United States (Washington, D.C.: Government Printing Office, 1910).

22.   Ruth Shackelford's database of working women in 1900 has expanded our ability to speculate and draw conclusions about these women and I thank her for that.

23.   Weiner, From Working Girl to Working Mother, 21-22; Tentler, Wage-Earning Women, 115.

24.   Weiner, From Working Girl to Working Mother, 22.

25.   Weiner, From Working Girl to Working Mother, 21. Meyerowitz also documents for Chicago that the lowest rate of living apart is by the native-born children of immigrant parents. Because the data base only supplies the birthplace of the worker herself, this hypothesis could not be tested for San Francisco. Meyerowitz, Women Adrift, 7.

26.   Leslie Tentler, Wage-Earning Women, 58-60; Dickinson, Role of Immigrant Women, 215.

27.   U.S. Census Office, Twelfth Census of the United States: 1900, Vol. 1, Part 1, 724-725; U.S. Census Bureau, Thirteenth Census of the United States: Abstract of the Census with Supplement for California, 593. Approximately the same percentage of women fell into the age categories delineated in 1900 and 1910.

28.   U.S. Census Bureau, Thirteenth Census of the United States: Abstract with Supplement of California, 593, 595.

29.   Diner, Erin's Daughters in America, 16-21, 48-51, 94-97, 103.

30.   Weiner, From Working Girl to Working Mother, 6; Joan Dickinson, Role of Immigrant Women, 44; Tentler, Wage-Earning Women, 139.

31.   U.S. Bureau of the Census, Thirteenth Census of the United States: 1910, 4:601; Dickinson, Role of Immigrant Women, 107,116.

32.   U.S. Bureau of the Census. Department of Commerce. Fourteenth Census of the United States: 1920, 11 vols. (Washington, D.C.: Government Printing Office, 1922-1923) 4:1230.

33.   Weiner, From Working Girl to Working Mother, 64-66; U.S. Bureau of the Census, Thirteenth Census of the United States, 1910, 4:601. U.S. Bureau of the Census, Fourteenth Census of the United States: 1920, 4:1230.

34.   U.S. Bureau of the Census, Thirteenth Census of the United States, 1910, 4:601; Weiner, From Working Girl to Working Mother, 28-9; Dickinson, Role of Immigrant Women in the U.S. Labor Force, 30; Tentler, Wage-Earning Women, 17-21,23-4; Issel and Cherny, San Francisco: 1865-1932, 55. Lucile Eaves noted that many of the industrial jobs that would have gone to women (and children) were filled by Chinese men who were imported to provide a pool of cheap labor. Many labor books and articles, including Eaves', were filled with virulent attacks on Asians. Eaves, A History of California Labor Legislation, University of California Publications in Economics, vol. 2 (Berkeley: University of California Press, 1910), 311.

35.   U.S. Bureau of the Census, Thirteenth Census of the United States, 4:601.

36.   Dorothy Sue Cobble, "Sisters in the Craft: Waitresses and Their Unions in the Twentieth Century," 2 vols. (Ph.D. dissertation, Stanford University, 1986), 526. The occupation would continue to become female-dominated, and by the 1970s, nine out of ten of those serving food commercially were women. These sharp increases also reflected the growth of the restaurant industry and the nation's rising tendency to "eat out." San Franciscans had already acquired this habit.

37.   U.S. Bureau of the Census, Thirteenth Census of the United States: 1910, 4:601; U.S. Bureau of the Census, Fourteenth Census of the United States: 1920, 4:1230.

38.   U.S. Bureau of the Census, Thirteenth Census of the United States: 1910, 4:601.

39.   U.S. Bureau of the Census, Thirteenth Census of the United States: 1910, 4: 600-601; State of California, Bureau of Labor Statistics, Fifteenth Biennial Report, 1911-12, (Sacramento: State Printing Office, 1912), 104-202. Only 38 male stenographers could be found out of all the firms and industries surveyed in the Fifteenth Biennial Report. Most of them worked in retail establishments and earned more than their female counterparts. On gender-based occupational segregation, see Kessler-Harris, Out To Work, 138-141, David W. Gordon, and others, Segmented Work, Divided Workers (Cambridge and New York: Cambridge University Press, 1982), 120-121, 150-152.

40.   U.S. Bureau of the Census, Thirteenth Census of the United States: Abstract of the Census with Supplement for California, 593; U.S. Bureau of the Census, Thirteenth Census of the United States: 1910, 4: 601.

41.   U.S. Bureau of the Census, Thirteenth Census of the United States: 1910, 4:601; Lucie Cheng Hirata, "Free, Indentured, Enslaved: Chinese Prostitutes in Nineteenth Century America," Signs 5(Autumn 1979): 3-29; Ruth Rosen, The Lost Sisterhood (Baltimore: The Johns Hopkins University Press, 1982), 139. These historians demonstrate that a high proportion of West Coast prostitutes were Chinese or Japanese. Due to the highly disproportionate number of Chinese women to men, and also to the fact that many Chinese women were sold into prostitution by their families in the homeland, it is likely that a significant number of Chinese women were sex workers. Lucie Cheng Hirata also documented that brothel owners forced nineteenth century prostitutes to spend their days as home-workers in the garment industry, providing them with additional profit. This fact was probably also hidden from the census pollsters.

42.   Tentler, Wage-Earning Women, 180-181.

43.   Sarah Eisenstein wrote of this self-defense of women's wage work and union consciousness in the early twentieth century. She concluded that ". . . working women of the period recognized the necessity to work and fought for the right to do so and under conditions roughly equal to those of men. In the process, they began to develop a rudimentary critique of the social and structural assumptions underlying the socially desired female life pattern. They also developed an appreciation of the value of friendship and association with other women in collective efforts." Sarah Eisenstein, Give Us Bread But Give Us Roses:Working Women's Consciousness in the United States, 1890 to the First World War (London: Routledge and Kegan Paul, 1983), 33.

44.   Jack London, "South of the Slot" in Strength of the Strong (New York: Macmillan Co., 1919), 34-59.

45.   Agnes Peterson's quote appeared in Susan B. Anthony's newspaper, The Revolution, 10 September,1868. Samples of the Women's Cooperative Printing Union are housed at the California Historical Society in San Francisco. The WCPU was incorporated with Judd Hicks, a printing firm, in the 1880s, after the WCTU's superintendent married Nelson Judd. Fire destroyed the business in 1901. When the shop reopened, Judd Hicks absorbed the WCPU. ending its existence as a separate entity. Barbara L. Grey, "One Woman's Struggle" (Independent study paper, City College of San Francisco, 1988), 11; San Francisco Chronicle, 4 September 1901. The National Typographical Union became an international union in 1869 when Canadian locals affiliated with it. George A. Tracy, A History of the Typographical Union (Indianapolis: International Typographical Union, 1913), 230.

46.   Miriam Allen deFord, They Were San Franciscans (Caldwell, ID: The Caxton Printers, Ltd., 1941), 136-145.

47.   Eaves, A History of California Labor Legislation, 312; Lillian Matthews, Women in the Trade Unions in San Francisco, 4-8; Jonathan Garlock, Guide to the Knights of Labor (Westport, Conn.: Greenwood Press, 1982), 25.

48.   Matthews, Women in Trade Unions in San Francisco, pp.88-94; see also Robert Edward Lee Knight, Industrial Relations in the San Francisco Bay Area, (Berkeley and Los Angeles: University of California Press, 1960), 63-4. Jefferson D. Pierce, an organizer sent by the AFL, aided this trend by encouraging unionization in semi-skilled and unskilled occupations that had been previously unorganized. Women's wage work obviously fell under this category. Olaf Tveitmoe, secretary of the Building Trades Council, castigated Pierce and the Labor Council for organizing these unions, which he termed "curious

ducklings". Tveitmoe claimed that unionizing unskilled workers unnecessarily stirred up labor unrest and created a group of pseudo-unions that were bound to fail. See Organized Labor, 22 June 1901.

49.   Diner, Erin's Daughters in America, 99-101; Michael Kazin, Barons of Labor: The San Francisco Building Trades and Union Power in the Progressive Era (Urbana and Chicago: University of Illinois Press, 1983), 23. For a detailed account of Yorke's life and his involvement in the labor movement, see Bernard Cornelius Cronin, Father Yorke and the Labor Movement in San Francisco (Washington, D.C.: Catholic University of America Press, 1943).

50.   Matthews, Women in Trade Unions in San Francisco, 11-14.

51.   Matthews, Women in Trade Unions in San Francisco, 11-14.

52.   Matthews, Women in Trade Unions in San Francisco, 15-16.

53.   Matthews, Women in Trade Unions in San Francisco, 15-17; California Bureau of Labor Statistics, Fifteenth Biennial Report, 133-134.

54.   Matthews, Women In Trade Unions in San Francisco, 38.

55.   Matthews, Women In Trade Unions in San Francisco, 78.

56.   Matthews, Women In Trade Unions in San Francisco, 78-80. These contract provisions also appeared in contracts in San Jose, Cleveland and Pittsburgh at this time. Cobble, "Sisters in the Craft," 298-301.

57.   Labor Clarion, 23 February 1906; Cobble, "Sisters of the Craft," 122-123.

58.   Matthews, Women In Trade Unions in San Francisco, 78-79. Mixer and Server (June 1911): 41, (July 1913): 46; U.S. Bureau of the Census, Thirteenth Census of the United States: 1910, 601.

59.   Cobble, "Sisters in the Craft," 1-4, 23-24, 527-528; H.S. Crocker Co., Crocker-Langley San Francisco Directory (San Francisco: H.S. Crocker Co., 1904), 1092.

60.   Matthews expressed these views in her surveys of the various women's unions in Women in Trade Unions in San Francisco, 10-88. Eaves, A History of California Labor Legislation, 317.

61.   Matthews, Women in Trade Unions in San Francisco, 10-85; Labor Clarion, 1 March 1912; Mixer and Server (June 1911): 41; (July 1913): 46.

62.   Kessler-Harris, Out To Work, 152.

63.   Knight, Industrial Relations in the San Francisco Bay Area, 1900-1918, 209-212. The Building Trades Council withdrew from the San Francisco Labor Council in 1900, but rejoined that body in 1910 following P.H. McCarthy's election. Robert W. Cherny and William Issel, San Francisco: Presidio, Port and Pacific Metropolis (San Francisco: Boyd & Fraser Pub. Co., 1981), 44. National figures for trade union growth show a similar trend toward expansion in membership during this period. Foster Rhea Dulles and Melvyn Dubofsky, Labor In America (Arlington Heights, Ill.: Harlan Davidson, Inc., 1984), 184-185, 196.

64.   Historian Edward Rowell credited the Union Labor Party's reign and Eugene Schmitz's mayoralty in particular with labor's high morale and organizational surge during the twentieth century's first decade. Schmitz refused to call out the police during a 1904 streetcar strike and a 1906 dispute between the United Shipping and Transport Association and the Sailors Union of the Pacific. Edward Rowell, "The Union Labor Party of San Francisco, 1901-1910" (Ph.D dissertation, University of California at Berkeley, 1928): 127-135. Edward Eaves also documents that Schmitz's mediation in 1902 resulted in a mutually agreeable contract between the Restaurant Keepers Association and the culinary unions. Edward Eaves, "A History of the Cooks' and Waiters' Unions of San Francisco" (Ph.D dissertation, University of California at Berkeley, 1930): 38-40; Jules Tygiel, " 'Where Unionism Holds Undisputed Sway' -- A Reappraisal of San Francisco's Union Labor Party," California History 62 (Fall 1983): 213. The following sources deal with the history of the Union Labor Party in detail: Walton Bean, Boss Ruef's San Francisco (Berkeley and Los Angeles, University of California Press, 1968) and Jules Tygiel, " 'Where Unionism Holds Undisputed Sway'", 196-215.

65.   Ira B. Cross, A History of the Labor Movement in California (Berkeley and Los Angeles: University of California Press, 1935), 135-142; Robert V. Ohlson, "The History of San Francisco Labor Council, 1892-1939" (M.A. thesis, University of California, Berkeley, 1940), 180-184; Cross, History of Labor Movement in California, 262-267; Lucile Eaves, History of California Labor Legislation, 5-6. For a more detailed account of anti-Asian racism in the labor movement, see Alexander Saxton, The Indispensable Enemy:Labor and the Anti-Chinese Movement in San Francisco (Berkeley and Los Angeles: University of California Press, 1971). Jules Becker's dissertation provides a look at the anti-Asian sentiment that pervaded the nation in this period. Jules Becker, "The Course of Exclusion: San Francisco Newspaper Coverage of Chinese and Japanese in the United States, 1882-1924" (Ph.D. dissertation, University of California, Berkeley, 1986). Most recently, Saxton documents the centrality of

racism nationally to the development of skilled craft unionism in the nineteenth century. Citing the California white working-class's virulent anti-Asian hostility in particular, Saxton concluded that "white racism in the society at large, and within the white labor force, contributed to the dominance of skilled craft unionism. But craft unionism in turn, defending its dominance, worked to extend and perpetuate the influence of white racism." Alexander Saxton, The Rise and Fall of the White Republic: Class Politics and Mass Culture in Nineteenth-Century America (New York: Verso, 1990), 293-319.

66.   Labor Clarion, 8 August 1907, 11 August 1911; "Proceedings of 1909 Convention," October 1, pp. 12-28, National Women's Trade Union League Papers (henceforth NWTUL), Microfilm Reel 19, Library of Congress, Washington, D.C.

67.   Matthews, Women in Trade Unions in San Francisco, 79; "Waitresses' Local 48 Constitution and Bylaws," n.d., San Francisco Labor Council Papers, Bancroft Library, University of California, Berkeley, CA. Waitresses' Unions nationally shared a distaste for "the yellow race," believing it "could not be assimilated in our social and economic surroundings." While some unions granted blacks membership in separate culinary locals or permitted to join as at-large members, Asians were universally barred. Like the San Francisco labor community, waitresses used the practice of "limiting" to reinforce unity. Cobble, "Sister in the Craft," 156-159, 117. Women in Trade Unions in San Francisco, 36. Matthews reproduced literature produced by the Anti-Jap Laundry League in the appendix of her study. Matthews, Women in Trade Unions in San Francisco, 95-100.

68.   Nancy Breen, "Did San Francisco Women Unionists Choose the Wrong Benchmark?" paper presented at the Southwest Labor Studies Conference annual meeting, Stockton, California, March, 1991. Breen's paper dealt with the subordinate role that women in the labor force and the labor movement occupied as a result of viewing Chinese and Japanese men as their chief job competition. They did not use white male wage rates and working conditions as their standard for equity but sought to improve their lot as part of a secondary work force. Consequently, their preoccupation with instituting racism, as well as a certain acceptance of women's position in the labor force, diverted them from the realization that they accepted second-class status as wage-earners.

69.   Coast Seamen's Journal, 4 October 1899; 1908-13 passim; 23 July 1913; 27 August 1913.

70.   Labor Clarion, 24 March 1911; 1908-11 passim. For a survey of attitudes toward women in the national labor press, see Ann Schofield, "Rebel

Girls and Union Maids: The Woman Question in the Journals of the AFL and IWW, 1905-1920," Feminist Studies 9 (Summer 1983): 335-358.

71.   Michael Kazin, "Barons of Labor: The San Francisco Building Trades, 1896-1920"(Ph.D. dissertation, Stanford University, 1983), 582-584, Kazin, Barons of Labor, 152. I use both Kazin's dissertation and the published book because the dissertation included a separate appendix on women and the labor movement in San Francisco that did not appear in the book Barons of Labor.

72.   Kazin, "Barons of Labor", 581. Kazin's information was confirmed by inspecting the Bureau of Labor Statistics tables on Hours and Wages for 1911-12. Indeed, the tables listed no women working in building trades jobs with the exception of office clericals. California Bureau of Labor Statistics, Fifteenth Biennial Report, 102-159.

73.   Matthews, Women in Trade Unions in San Francisco, 13-14, 57, 44.

74.   Louise Ploeger, "Trade Unionism Among the Women of San Francisco, 1920" (M.A. thesis, University of California, Berkeley, 1920), 2.

75.   Matthews, Women in Trade Unions in San Francisco, 78, 70, 40.

76.   Eleanor Flexner, Century of Struggle (Cambridge: Belknap Press, 1959; New York: Atheneum, 1973), 74, 76; Carol Hymowitz and Michaele Weissman, A History of Women in America (New York: Bantam Books, 1978), 94; Barbara Wertheimer, We Were There (New York: Pantheon Books,1977), 103-105; Kessler-Harris, Out To Work, 52.

77.   For more complete accounts of the Working Women's Association, see Diane Balser, Sisterhood and Solidarity (Boston: South End Press, 1987), pp. 53-85; Philip Foner, Women and the American Labor Movement (New York: Free Press, 1979), 145-154; and Grey, "One Woman's Struggle."

78.   Wertheimer, We Were There: The Story of Working Women in America (New York: Pantheon, 1977), 180-191 for a good brief account of women in the Knights of Labor.

79.   For a short but instructive description of the WEIU, see Karen Blair, The Clubwoman as Feminist (New York: Holmes and Meier Publishers, Inc., 1980), 73-91. Foner, Women and the American Labor Movement, 179-181; Reda Davis, California Women: a Guide to Their Politics 1885-1911 (San Francisco: n.p., 1967), 44; "The Women's Educational and Industrial Union," (n.p.: n.d.), Women's Educational and Industrial Union papers, California Historical Society, San Francisco, California.

80.   Foner, Women and the American Labor Movement, 292-3, 331; Ellen DuBois, "Working Women, Class Relations, and Suffrage Militance: Harriot Stanton Blatch and the New York Women Suffrage Movement, 1894-1909," Journal of American History 74 (June 1987): 37. Maud Nathan notes that San Francisco Bay Area woman reformers formed a local branch of the NCL in 1909, called the Bay Cities Consumer's League. The BCCL investigated conditions in local department stores and campaigned for minimum wage legislation for women, which passed in 1913 over the objections of women trade unionists. In general, however, the group seems to have kept a low profile and did not acquire the crusading reputation of the NCL in the East. Maud Nathan, The Story of an Epoch-Making Movement (Garden City, NY: Doubleday, Page and Co., 1926), 142-145. For a broader discussion of the campaign for the minimum wage law for women and minors, see Rebecca Mead, "Trade Unionism and Political Activity Among San Francisco Wage-Earning Women, 1900-1922" (M.A. thesis: San Francisco State University, 1991).

81.   For an overview of women's labor activity in the last half of the nineteenth century, see Wertheimer, We Were There, 151-261; Foner, Women and the American Labor Movement, 122-255.

82.   For more complete histories of the National Women's Trade Union League during this period, see Gladys Boone, The Women's Trade Union Leagues in Great Britain and the United States (New York: Columbia University Press, 1942), 43-110; Wertheimer, We Were There, 267-317; Foner, Women and the American Labor Movement, 290-345; Nancy Schrom Dye, As Sisters and As Equals (Columbia: University of Missouri Press, 1980). For a brief but incisive analysis of the relationship between the NWTUL and main-stream feminism, see Robin M. Jacoby, "The Women's Trade Union League and American Feminism" in Cantor and Laurie, ed., Class, Sex and the Woman Worker, 203-24. When the current women's movement was young, the following article criticized the average middle-class feminist's inability to work with laboring women at the turn of the century, citing the tensions within the NWTUL as a situation that should not be perpetuated in late twentieth-century feminism; Susan Reverby, "The Labor and Suffrage Movements: A View of Working-Class Women in the in the 20th Century" in Liberation Now! (New York: Dell Books, 1971), 94-101.

83.   Jacoby, "The Women's Trade Union League and American Feminism", 203; Ellen DuBois, "Working Women, Class Relations, and Suffrage Militance," 46.

84.   Schrom Dye, As Equals and As Sisters, 1-4, 31-36, 117, 150-151. While the organization's priority became protective legislation, that did not mean that the New York NWTUL became less working-class. On the contrary, the bulk

of active members were union members and organizers such as Rose Schneiderman. However, the group lost its grass-root character. Demoralized by the antagonism of male unionists, a hostile post-war political climate, the uphill nature of unionizing women and the withdrawal of most middle-class allies, the organization was reduced to a paid staff which spent most of its time lobbying the New York State legislature to enact protective labor legislation for women. It survived until 1955.

85.   A San Francisco branch of the WTUL was briefly noted by Elizabeth A. Payne, Margaret Dreier Robins' biographer, to be "weak and lonely." Little else is known about it. Frances Noel founded a Los Angeles chapter in 1914. Only after World War I did a branch materialize in Seattle. Elizabeth A. Payne, Reform, Labor and Feminism: Margaret Dreier Robins and the Women's Trade Union League (Urbana and Chicago: University of Illinois Press, 1988), 49; Sherry Katz, Frances Nacke Noel and 'Sister Movements': Socialism, Feminism and Trade Unionism," California History 67 (September 1988): 184-186; Greenwald, "Working-Class Feminism and the Family Wage," 131.

86.   Cross, History of Labor Movement in California, 338; Knight, Industrial Relations in San Francisco Bay Area, 47. The laundry work hours statute was declared unconstitutional later that year.

87.   Matthews, Women in Trade Unions in San Francisco, 81.

88.   Eaves, History of California Labor Legislation, 313; Joan M. Jenson and Gloria R. Lothrup, California Women: A History (San Francisco: Boyd and Fraser Publishing Co., 1987), 58; "Proceedings of the 1909 Convention," September 29, pp. 21-22, NWTUL Papers.

89.   Dorothy Sue Cobble, "Rethinking Troubled Relations Between Women and Unions: Craft Unionism and Female Activism" Feminist Studies 16 (Fall 1990): 519-548.

90.   Nancy F. Cott, The Grounding of Modern Feminism (New Haven: Yale University Press, 1987), 4-5.

CHAPTER 2

FIGHTING FOR JUSTICE VERSUS SEARCHING FOR ORDER:
CLASS CONFLICT IN THE CALIFORNIA WOMAN SUFFRAGE
MOVEMENT, 1896-1909

In 1896, California voters defeated a proposition granting women the right
to vote. While southern California and the rural areas supported the measure,
San Francisco Bay area voters decisively trounced the proposed amendment to
the state constitution. Stunned by the failure, California suffrage organizations
limped away from the campaign and effectively went into hibernation for five
years. The California Woman Suffrage Association, the state-wide coordinating
structure, held no state conventions during this period. Only nine local suffrage
clubs survived the debacle, most of them in San Francisco, and fewer than a
hundred state activists continued to promote suffrage during this period. The
state body constructed during the campaign dwindled to a mere skeleton.[1]

California's slump following the 1896 election was not unique.
Nationally, the suffrage movement entered a fourteen-year period dubbed "the
doldrums," during which no state enfranchised women. This fallow stretch was
exacerbated by a leadership crisis in the National American Woman Suffrage
Association which followed the 1896 defeat and Susan B. Anthony's decline as
a visible steward of the movement prior to her death in 1906. Anna Howard
Shaw, NAWSA President from 1906 to 1915, lacked the dynamism and sense of

direction needed to reinvigorate the organization. In the midst of an era of reform and political action, NAWSA seemed, in comparison, becalmed.[2]

The process of revitalizing the suffrage movement began at the state and local level, as the leadership of suffrage groups restructured the clubs and devised new strategies. Concurrently, working-class women rose as a new source of membership and of tactics. In particular, female unionists verbalized an interest in woman suffrage and attempted to join forces with the reform-minded middle-class women who had been the backbone of the movement since its inception. In San Francisco, union women sought an alliance with reform suffragists of the San Francisco Equal Suffrage League in 1907 to advance the suffrage cause. An examination of their tense, fugue-like relationship revealed a series of ideological differences which hindered their ability to work in the same grouping and eventually dictated the need for a separate organization for the union women. These differences originated with the nature of the leadership of the 1896 California woman suffrage campaign and carried through the first years of the twentieth century movement in the Golden State.

Daniel W. Rodes noted in his history of California woman suffrage that temperance adherents largely comprised the leadership of the 1896 campaign. Many Progressive-era middle-class reformers viewed liquor as the chief agent for moral, spiritual, and economic degeneration. They blamed alcohol consumption for many of the problems of lower-class communities, such as poverty, family violence, malnutrition, poor hygiene, and promiscuity, and they believed that the only answer was the legal restriction of its sale.[3]

The woman suffrage and temperance movements shared certain leaders and strands of ideology and strategy from the mid-nineteenth century. Frances Willard, the Woman's Christian Temperance Union's (WCTU) most illustrious national president, called for women to "Do Everything" on behalf of stamping out drunkenness. The women's vote ranked high on her list of priorities and Willard promoted woman suffrage through the WCTU's Franchise Department in the 1880s and 1890s. Through the vote, Willard surmised, women could tip the balance and bring in prohibition.[4]

In California, women participated in a so-called Crusade in 1874 to persuade male citizens in their towns and districts to vote for no-license ordinances, which prohibited the sale of liquor licenses. Suffragists like Sallie Hart campaigned heartily in San Jose and San Leandro for a local dry option. In his history of the California prohibition movement, Gilman M. Ostrander speculated that this crusade "was as much a woman suffrage demonstration as it was a temperance campaign." The women's message implied that if they had the franchise, they would vote for no-license laws, and that their vote would make the difference.[5]

While ties existed between the temperance and suffrage movements, however, each carefully avoided strong associations with the other. Because of their fledgling status, both feared alienating supporters and draining energy away from their particular issue. Neither woman suffrage nor women's temperance organizations in California in the 1870s endorsed each others' issues. The two movements were connected, but not synonymous. In 1896, Susan B. Anthony convinced Frances Willard to hold that year's National WCTU convention outside California so as not to affect adversely the woman suffrage measure on the ballot that year.[6]

This guise, however, did little to fool the liquor interests, who realized that the small army of women working to win votes for women was largely composed of temperance leaders and activists. Mrs. Sturtevant Peet, the California WCTU president, submitted a petition of 15,000 signatures to the state legislature in 1893 which helped stimulate debate on the issue. Mary McHenry Keith noted that the WCTU proved to be "a powerful ally" in the 1896 effort and was largely responsible for the "well-organized army of workers" which campaigned for woman suffrage that year. The proposed constitutional amendment lost and evidence indicates that the liquor interests played a large role in its defeat.[7]

Carrie Chapman Catt, president of the National American Woman Suffrage Association (NAWSA) and Susan B. Anthony's immediate successor, visited California in 1901 in an attempt to raise the morale of her troops there. The effort succeeded. State leaders recommitted themselves to the cause and began the process of rebuilding the organization. The NAWSA dispatched organizer Gail Laughlin to California to give its western sisters a hand.[8] By 1905, the California Woman Suffrage Association boasted of fifty-two new clubs in addition to the revival of twenty clubs from the 1896 effort. The federation also renamed itself the California Equal Suffrage Association (CESA) in an attempt to appeal to sympathetic men.[9]

The bulk of leaders after 1900 were drawn from the membership of California's women's club movement. Many of these clubs were a direct outgrowth of the 1896 campaign and mainly involved themselves in civic improvement and humane services. While temperance continued to be a concern for some of these women, it lost its predominance and became one of a number of reform interests. A prime example of this type of activism was the California Club of San Francisco. Formed in 1898 by members of the Forty-First District Suffrage Club, the Club hoped to promote the notion of women as responsible and vital citizens through participation in San Francisco's public affairs.[10]

During the first year of its existence, the California Club organized the one of the first public playgrounds on the Pacific coast, located at Bush and Hyde Streets in San Francisco, and financed its operation for three years. It lobbied for and won the first municipally-funded playground in California and is believed to have started the save-the-redwoods movement. After 1900, the Club promoted an anti-race track law, conducted a consumer's boycott of stores which did not treat their "shopgirls" fairly or sold clothing made in sweatshops, and sponsored public art and music presentations through an Outdoor Art League.[11]

The California Club also sought to draw in women not previously identified with the suffrage movement and to educate them about the need for the franchise. Their purpose in this "indirect agitation" was to make woman suffrage more acceptable and desirable to the general public.[12]

More politically-inclined members like Lillian Harris Coffin grew impatient with the Club's indirect means. She shifted her attention to the reborn suffrage movement and, in 1906, Coffin founded the San Francisco Equal Suffrage League, an amalgamation of several local suffrage clubs. The League elected Mary Gamage, another clubwoman, as its president. Later that year, the California Equal Suffrage Association named Coffin head of its State Central Committee. In addition, fellow California Club members Mary Sperry, Elizabeth Lowe Watson, and Alice Park held office as CESA President, Resolutions Committee Chair, and Recording Secretary, respectively. Century Club[13] founder Ellen Clark Sargent, who had been a part of the California woman suffrage movement since its inception in 1869, chaired the CESA Literature Committee.[14]

These women probably brought their compatriots in the clubs into contact with the various suffrage organizations at the local and state level. By 1907, Mary McHenry Keith reported that over 5,000 California clubwomen endorsed suffrage. While the figure cannot be documented, it demonstrates that suffragists were anxious to bind clubwomen to the movement.[15]

As Karen Blair has noted in The Clubwoman as Feminist, clubwomen at the turn of the century constituted one of many elements of Progressive Era reformers.[16] It is likely that they shared many characteristics common to Progressives, such as the desire for social harmony, the minimization of class differences, and an abhorrence for conflict, which they perceived as irrational and destructive. Indeed, this social view was common to many Progressive era reformers, as described by Robert Wiebe in his ground-breaking synthesis, The

Search for Order.[17]   This reform consciousness would clash with the very
different assumptions held by union women active in the suffrage movement.

By 1907, union women worked for the vote alongside other suffragists in
the San Francisco Equal Suffrage League.   Louise LaRue, secretary of
Waitresses Local 48, claimed the female unionists joined "with the National
Woman's Suffrage League [sic] in San Francisco and got along fine with them;
we endorsed everything they did."[18]

While neither middle-class suffragists nor union sources documented just
when the unionists allied themselves with the Equal Suffrage League, the union
women probably participated in the effort to secure passage of a woman suffrage
resolution introduced in March of 1907 by State Assembly representative Grove
L. Johnson of Sacramento. Johnson's bill squeaked through the Assembly on the
second ballot but failed in the Senate by two votes.   The bill won the
endorsement of the Union Labor Party and the California Federation of Labor.[19]

After the turn of the century, liquor continued to be an issue for
suffragists. While the temperance and prohibition movement did attract some
mainstream feminists, anti-liquor attitudes also seemed to spring from a
resentment against the political power wielded by the liquor interests. In a 1911
interview in the San Francisco Examiner, Mary McHenry Keith fumed, "The
'Saloon in Politics' has for fifteen years been successful in preventing any
legislation . . . allowing this question of woman suffrage to get out before the
people." Keith also reported that a San Francisco State Senator informed her
that if she could convince all the saloon, hotel, and restaurant keepers, liquor
dealers, and other purveyors of alcoholic beverages in his district to support
woman suffrage, he would vote in kind.[20]

In 1908, California Club leaders backed a proposed effort to raise license
fees for saloons in San Francisco to $1000. A spokeswoman from the club
stated that "all women" supported the measure, and that reducing the number of
saloons would decrease the chance that young women would come into contact

with hard liquor.[21] In July of 1909, the WCTU organized a Congress of Reform in Berkeley. The roster of speakers contained a large dose of suffrage leaders including Mary Sperry, Ellen Clark Sargent, Lillian Coffin, and Mary McHenry Keith of the California Equal Suffrage Association. Elizabeth Gerberding, future president of the Woman Suffrage Party, was also featured; she represented the Citizens League for Justice.[22]

Though suffragists again feared a close identification with the temperance movement and a resulting backlash from the politically influential liquor industry, historic ties, and sympathy persisted between the two movements. Many who worked for woman suffrage, both nationally and locally, joined other Progressives in decrying the effects of alcohol itself as well as the role of liquor interests in politics.

In contrast, beer, wine, and spirits frequently occupied a central place in many immigrant and working-class communities. Many men and women made their living brewing, fermenting, or distilling alcohol, and bottling, transporting and vending it. Many German, Irish, and Italian San Franciscans who worked in the industries and consumed the product regarded alcohol both as a means of support and a part of their culture.

The saloon was often a male social and political center. The average San Francisco saloon offered card games, billiards, gambling machines, and other games of chance. In addition, many served free or cheap lunches, lent clients money or extended credit and afforded a club where men could meet their friends, sing, and, on occasion, even sleep. Ward-heelers could contact the men of their precinct, build a political following over glasses of beer, and distribute political favors. Historian Jon Kingsdale reported that San Francisco saloons were so plentiful that in 1915 there was one for every 218 people. In most cities, working class districts housed the highest proportion of drinking establishments to the extent that many had one for every fifty adult males.[23]

The labor movement held ambivalent attitudes toward saloons and drinking. Union officials often bemoaned liquor's ability to dull the fighting spirit of local members. On the other hand, most unions were fiercely anti-prohibitionist. San Francisco labor unions resisted the 1908 higher license measure, claiming that the law could put breweries out of business and cost hundreds of men their jobs. In 1909, the Labor Clarion announced that the San Francisco Labor Council opposed prohibition and any legislation designed to limit the issuance of liquor licenses. Specifically, it went before the state legislature to condemn the Local Option Bill which would permit each county to place no-license measures on the ballot.[24]

Women unionists may also have had mixed feeling about alcohol and saloons. Nationally, women union members resented that some union locals held their membership meetings in saloons which were held to be unfit places for women. This was not the case in San Francisco, judging from the roster of labor organizations in the Labor Clarion from 1907-1911. Unions either had their own halls, rented them, or held meetings in the buildings which housed the San Francisco Labor Council and the Building Trades Council.[25] Some of these women undoubtably witnessed the effect of alcoholism on individuals and families. However, labor agitators like Mary Harris, the United Mine Workers' organizer more commonly known as "Mother Jones," maintained that temperance supporters only wanted to ban liquor in order to squeeze more work out of toilers. She argued that closing saloons deprived workingmen of their own club and denied them one of the few pleasures they had. Because of life's trials, Jones mused, "It's a wonder we are not all drunk all of the time."[26]

In 1906 San Francisco Waitresses Local 48 successfully opposed a local law which would have denied them work in establishments which served liquor. Temperance activists sponsored a similar bill on the state level in 1911 and Local 48 spoke out again. Louise LaRue warned that "such a law . . . would have injured the girls all over the state and particularly in this city, as nearly all the restaurants serve liquor." To these women, liquor consumption was less a moral issue than an economic one. They did not wish to be cut out of work in the restaurants with bars. This incident also represented one of many efforts by waitresses nationally to preserve or open up jobs in workplaces selling alcoholic beverages and to serve liquor and beer themselves. These working women resented the efforts of moral crusaders to enact these reforms instead of concentrating on economic and social advances.[27]

Liquor was also a source of income for Local 48. The waitresses served liquor at the benefit ball for their sick and death benefit. This fund provided expenses for medical care for Local 48 members and paid for the burial costs of poor members. The bar alone raised $600 to $800 for the fund, money the waitresses could ill-afford to turn away. Despite the good works this fund provided, the fact that Local 48 sold alcohol at its affairs "provoked considerable disapproval" according to Lillian Matthews. Similarly, middle-class women rarely approached waitresses with any type of aid because of their association with alcohol and, some imagined, prostitution. Louise Ploeger identified this as a continuing problem between the two classes of women in 1920.[28]

Another point of difference between these two groups of women lay in the reformers' belief in suffrage's potential to transform the lives of working women versus the unionists' equally strong commitment to union organizing for the same reason. Women reformers and suffragists promised that the vote and resultant protective legislation would provide women with the greatest protection and rights on the job. When asked in 1905 how Los Angeles female laundry workers could secure a nine-hour day, Susan B. Anthony replied, "We are heartily in favor of women's trade unions but you will never get full justice until you have the ballot."[29] San Francisco union women dissented. United Garment Workers' Union President Sarah Hale challenged reformers to "expend one-half the energy (you) are now wasting to institute organization" if they truly wished to benefit working women. Matthews similarly observed about women unionists,

"To them, the trade union with its power to educate the worker and to make effective the demands of the worker offers the proper medium for the solution of their difficulties." Seven years later, Louise Ploeger concurred on this matter in a study done as a follow-up to Matthews's work. While the vote and legislation were important tools to improve women's work lives, Ploeger described them as incomplete without the power of collective bargaining.[30]

Tension between reform and union suffragists came to a head in the spring of 1907. San Francisco was still in turmoil following the earthquake and fire when, on May 5, more than 1500 members of the Carmen's Union struck the United Railroads, the corporation that owned the franchise for San Francisco's transit system. Patrick Calhoun, president of the United Railroad, refused to consider granting the streetcar drivers the eight-hour day or raising wages to three dollars per day. The union responded to Calhoun's uncompromising stand with an overwhelming vote by the union membership for a strike.[31]

On the strike's first day, no streetcars rumbled on the rails which connected the San Francisco's residential districts with the financial and industrial areas downtown. Residents, out for Sunday church or amusement, either walked or hailed wagons and carriages willing to give them a lift for a fee. That same day, scabs hired by Calhoun from James Farley's infamous strikebreaking agency quietly entered San Francisco, prepared to get the streetcars rolling at any cost.[32]

The following day United Railroad erected barbed wire barriers around the carbarns, which housed Farley's goons. Hundreds of strikers, sympathizers and spectators gathered at the barns in anticipation of an attempt by the company to resume transit service. No cars left the barns, however, and the day passed without incident.[33]

"Bloody Tuesday," as unionists dubbed May 7, dawned as unionists again took their positions outside the carbarns. On this morning, strikebreakers drove six cars out of the barn with private armed guards on board. Enraged, the unionists barraged the cars with rocks and bricks and traded shots with the guards. One elderly female sympathizer reportedly lay down on the tracks to block the cars' way with her body.[34]

In the wake of the melee, two unidentified men were shot to death and at least twenty others sustained injuries in the "street-car war."[35] Chief of Police Jeremiah Dinnan and the labor community placed the blame for the battle on gun-happy strikebreakers, an opinion that the usually pro-labor San Francisco Examiner echoed. The San Francisco Chronicle compared the day's events to the "lawless days of the 1850s," when the 1856 murder of San Francisco Bulletin editor James King of William sparked the formation of a Committee of Vigilance. Thus began the most violent strike in pre-World War I San Francisco and probably the bloodiest streetcar strike in the nation's history.[36]

The San Francisco Labor Council had initially hesitated in backing the Carmen's impulse to strike and instead promoted conciliation. "Bloody Tuesday," however, converted the Council to a pro-strike position. Shortly thereafter, the Council resolved to boycott the scab-run transit lines. "Neither the tens of thousands of loyal union men and women of San Francisco, nor the members of their families, nor sympathizers outside the union ranks, will ride in Calhoun's cars until he has made peace with the Street Carmen's Union," the Council proclaimed. The Labor Council also vowed to fine all unionists found riding the streetcars. Many individual unions followed suit. The Council also pleaded with unionists to refrain from protesting at the carbarns in the interest of public safety.[37]

At the height of the strike, Father Peter Yorke, labor's priest, responded to those San Franciscans who complained that the strike inconvenienced them or who decried the militance of the Carmen's Union. He bellowed, "We would like to ask those soft-hearted and soft-headed people who snivel over strikes and weep for the miseries inflicted on them by workingmen . . . what consideration have the workingmen ever received from their employers that was not forced?"[38]

While no succeeding day matched the ferocity of "Bloody Tuesday's," the scab-driven railway continued to be targeted by unionists and their allies for sabotage and skirmishes with the strikebreakers. Hundreds of riders suffered injuries due to this clash of forces, as well as the inexperience of the imported drivers.[39]

Despite the Labor Council's apparent enthusiasm, the boycott failed. Four months into the strike, the Labor Council called off the boycott, tacitly admitting that the Carmen were losing. Sapped of concrete union support, the strike slowly collapsed, ending in March 1908. Soon afterward, the Carmen's Union folded.[40]

Interestingly, the press gave significant attention to the role of women during the strike and boycott. The Chronicle was the first to report, on May 9, that women along the route of some streetcars waved and cheered the strikebreakers from their windows. By the next day, both the Chronicle and the more labor-oriented Examiner disclosed that female residents of the middle-class Western Addition and Richmond districts, as well as women along Sutter Street, presented cakes and flowers to the scabs, blew them kisses, and treated them like heroes. According to the Examiner, these acts infuriated pro-labor observers who cursed the women.[41]

When the first women passengers boarded the streetcars on May 11, one paper treated their maiden voyage as a major news event. The Chronicle filled page 2 of the next day's edition with pictures of these women, some with children, braving pro-union crowds to defy the boycott. The two cars depicted originated in the Western Addition and traveled to Market Street and the financial district.[42]

Women who stood by the strike were no less vocal and active. In addition to the woman who risked her life by blocking the tracks, female compatriots of the strikers jeered the strikebreakers and joined male unionists in pelting them with debris as streetcar service resumed. The Examiner identified some of these women as "telephone girls," telephone operators who were also on strike at that time for better wages and union recognition.[43]

On May 13, women living at the post-earthquake refugee Richmond Camp on the corner of 13th Avenue (now Funston Avenue) and California Street attacked streetcars with "missiles" and occupied the tracks with babies in their arms. Police arrested one participant during the protest.[44]

Waitress's Union Local 48 joined the unions which fined their members for disregarding the streetcar boycott. Any member found on a streetcar paid a $20 penalty, a sizable amount for anyone at that time, much less a working woman. In June, Local 48 collected ten cents per week from its members and, in August, each member was assessed an additional twenty-five cents in order to contribute to the nearly $300,000 raised by the labor community for strike support. The Steam Laundry Workers Union also passed a resolution declaring support for the strike and boycott.[45]

According to Louise LaRue, the unionists in the Equal Suffrage League had earlier sought to bolster the ties between the mainstream suffragists and themselves by supporting their actions. When the streetcar strike began, then, the unionists expected reciprocal aid for the issues they deemed important. That aid was not forthcoming, as middle- and upper-class reform suffragists actively opposed the strike and boycott. When pressed to explain why they would not observe the boycott, LaRue reported that the reform feminists agreed with critics who argued that "it was not the right time." They charged that the unionists were "wrong" in promoting the strike. LaRue retorted that she saw little "wrong" with "walking back and forth." Remonstrating with her fair-weather allies, she held out the condition that "they would have to stay with us and be friends with us even if we were wrong . . . but if they couldn't stick to us when we were wrong, we didn't want them when we were right."[46]

Because of their commitment to their brothers in the labor movement and to union principles of solidarity, unionists involved in the suffrage movement became enraged when their reformist sisters ignored the plight of the Carmen's Union. Judging from the newspaper reports and from the knowledge that many Progressive era reformers found labor conflict intolerable, some of those women probably hailed the effort to break the strike and quell the upheaval. "So you can just imagine how we felt about it. . . . We had to pull out," LaRue remarked when she reported the incident.[47]

Lack of sympathy for labor struggles was not a given for all women reformers of the period, however. In New York, in a remarkable display of solidarity, middle and upper class women joined thousands of women garment workers on picket lines in 1909 to protest miserable wages and working conditions at shirtwaist factories. During the strike's thirteen-week duration, hundreds of strikers and their well-heeled allies were beaten and arrested. Other women donated generously towards bail money for those jailed and to a relief fund for those without other resources during the strike. While the strike itself produced few permanent gains for the shirtwaist makers, it solidified bonds between wage-earning women and their Progressive counterparts. Aside from the fact that women reformers probably had an easier time identifying with strikers who were daughters, wives, and mothers like themselves, many held local membership in the organizations with a history of championing the rights of working women, such as the Women's Trade Union League and the National Consumers League. No comparable organizations existed in San Francisco at this time with the same type of broad membership base and popular appeal as those on the East Coast.[48]

In reviewing the concerns of the union women and their middle-class counterparts, it appears that other problems along with the dispute over union tactics came into play over the issue of the boycott. LaRue also alluded to a more basic reason that the mainstream suffragists spurned the boycott--they simply did not _want_ to walk. She explained that "some of those women were very wealthy, and some of their husbands were middle class merchants, and many of them objected to walking." Why should such ladies walk if they did not have to? LaRue intimates that class attitudes and more leisured lives inclined the middle-class women against walking.[49]

In addition to LaRue's perception, another factor which discouraged upper-strata women from walking lay in the distance of their homes from commercial San Francisco. Most middle-class families in San Francisco at the turn of the century resided in the Western Addition and Richmond districts. These neighborhoods grew up as a direct consequence of streetcar access. Residents depended on mass transit to convey them to their jobs, to the major downtown shopping area, and to the multitudinous halls of entertainment. Indeed, the two streetcar lines described in the May 12 Chronicle article originated in the Western Addition.[50]

While public transportation ran on most major streets in the working-class Mission district, work and recreation tended to be closer to home for these San Franciscans. Mission families and their lower working-class neighbors in the South-of-Market area probably relied less on trollies, as sports arenas, dance and music halls, and workplaces honeycombed these grittier locales. Walking was more of a daily reality and less of an onerous chore or stigmatizing act. Indeed, on their wages some residents could not afford streetcar fares; many of these would have been women. Aside from the union issue, then, class influenced residential patterns and streetcar patronage and, therefore, determined support for the boycott.[51]

The San Francisco graft prosecutions of 1906-1910 provided the final nail in the coffin of the relationship between reform and union suffragists. A colorful episode in the city's history, the trials have afforded historians an opportunity to explore such diverse issues as machine politics, progressive-era reform, and the role of class and ethnicity in politics. However, women's involvement in the trials has received only minor mention; it deserves more attention. A cadre of San Francisco middle-class women made a significant contribution towards promoting the graft trials and disseminating the spirit of reform during this period. These women gained prior experience in reform and political organizing through their membership in women's clubs and through their activity in the suffrage movement.   Galvanized by their concern that the graft trials were foundering and that the grafters would not be brought to justice, these women turned their attention and their expertise to this pressing issue. In doing so, they won the enmity of union women who opposed or disparaged the graft prosecution.

In 1901, San Franciscans elected Union Labor Party (ULP) candidate Eugene Schmitz as their mayor.   Catalyzed by city police protection of strikebreakers during a violent 1901 waterfront strike, a hodge-podge of politically inexperienced unionists founded the Union Labor Party. Abraham Ruef, an opportunist who had failed to carve out a fiefdom for himself in the Republican Party, immediately saw the potential of such a group. Ruef descended upon the ULP with a small body of pro-union men recruited from the Republican Party, a coherent platform, and an attractive mayoral candidate.   Handsome, engaging, of Irish and German parentage, and president of the Musicians' Union, Schmitz easily bested his two opponents.   The immigrant, working-class, South-of-Market district provided him with the bulk of his support. Schmitz and other Union Labor Party candidates again emerged victorious in the municipal elections of 1903 and 1905, reaffirming their solid working-class backing.[52]

In late 1906, a grand jury indicted Mayor Schmitz and "Boss" Ruef for accepting bribes from a number of corporations which had received franchises to operate city railroad lines, a telephone service, and gas and electric service. While most of the members of the San Francisco Board of Supervisors were also implicated, they received immunity in exchange for their testimony which incriminated Ruef and Schmitz. Following Schmitz's conviction and sentencing, several acting mayors served out the term of the deposed mayor.   San Franciscans then elected Democrat E.R. Taylor, dean of Hastings College of

Law, as his permanent replacement in November 1907. Local suffrage leaders played an active role in his campaign.[53]

Because the prosecution's long-term goal was to punish those who had proffered bribes as well as those who had accepted them, indictments against corporate officials from Home Telephone, Pacific State Telephone and Telegraph Co., the United Railroads and Pacific Gas and Electric soon followed. The trials were dramatic, righteous spectacles that rated a high level of press coverage.[54]

Initially the novelty and purpose of the trials generated a impressive degree of curiosity and excitement. By 1908, however, public interest flagged as the trials ground into their second year, Schmitz's conviction was overturned on appeal, juries acquitted United Railroad Chief Counsel Tirey Ford three times, and Ruef's first trial resulted in a hung jury. Frustrated by rising public apathy and hostility, a group of professionals and clergymen were jolted into action when an anti-prosecution assailant dynamited a key witness's house. Led by the Reverend C.N. Lathrop, these men recognized the need for a citizen's action group which could rally support for the prosecution. To that end, they launched the Citizens' League of Justice (CLJ) in June, 1908.[55]

The Women's Branch of the CLJ, founded in September of 1908, was to be its auxiliary. Composed of energetic women who had been active in the women's club and suffrage movement, however, the Women's Branch was not about to accept back seat status. Elizabeth Gerberding, Women's Branch president and Century Club member, captained the group and steered its course into the main channel of the CLJ's activity.[56]

Women from the Century and California Clubs quickly assumed leadership positions in the Woman's Branch. Century Club founder Ellen C. Sargent became Honorary President. After serving as temporary chair, Katherine Hittell became a "District Chairman" [sic]. Hittel belonged to both clubs. Other Century Club members included Mary S. Sperry and Club president Margaret Foster. The California Club contributed Lillian Harris Coffin, president Mrs.

J.W. Orr, and Alice Park. Park also belonged to the Palo Alto Women's Club. Mary H. Gamage of the Daughters of California Pioneers Society entertained League meetings in her home. Mrs. J.W. Orr also served as Vice President of the California Federation of Women's Clubs. Gerberding, Sargent, Sperry, Coffin, Gamage, and Park were all major leaders of the California woman suffrage movement.[57]

During the first year of the Branch's existence, it took on the responsibility of one of the League's main functions--attendance at the graft trials. Union Labor Party followers were packing the hearings, jeering the prosecution and attempting to influence the proceedings by verbal intimidation and by their presence. Male members of the League were unwilling or unable to spend time away from their businesses to counter these tactics. It was up to the women to pick up the torch.[58]

This was no mean feat. Because of the raucous atmosphere, the courtroom was not considered a fit place for women. Elizabeth Gerberding, the Woman's Branch president, noted that the women's initial entrance into court caused "a sensation." They appeared in court day after day, ignoring insults and jeers from the defendants' corner; proudly wearing "the blue button of the League, not aggressively, but fearlessly for the sake of the example it may serve."[59] Gerberding asked women to recruit their friends, fellow church-goers, and clubmembers to the Women's Branch. She also admonished Branch members not to "feed the enemy" or patronize those businesses supporting the trial defendants, but only those "who stood for the right." Gerberding counselled mothers to use the defendants as an object lesson of the consequences of corruption to their children and to teach young ones that all morality was absolute and based on fundamental Christian doctrine. They were to disabuse their children of the notion that one set of morals applied to the home and another applied to the business world and government.[60]

The clubwomen had further incentive to bash the grafters. California Club members still harbored a grudge against Mayor Schmitz for refusing to appoint a woman to the school board in 1902. A delegation from the Club met with Schmitz on the matter and he reportedly told the women that such an act was not in the interest of the school system. This incident must have riled the women for Mary McHenry Keith included it as a pertinent event in her history of California suffrage.[61]

While Women's Branch members witnessed Ruef's conviction and sentencing in December of 1908, the jury acquitted another key defendant in the spring of 1909 and public interest in the trials waned again. By the time of the WCTU Women's Reform Congress that July, Elizabeth Gerberding became convinced that the women of the CLJ must champion politicians who could renew the momentum needed to propel the trials to their just and moral conclusion. "While the League of Justice is nonpolitical, its members must perforce be interested in politics. It is essential that upright honest men be elected to office." When Chief Prosecutor Francis Heney decided to run for district attorney, the Woman's Branch reorganized into the California Women's Heney Club and jumped into the campaign with both feet.[62]

While mass meetings attracted attention to the campaign and made the women's work well known, "home meetings and personal contact" were the hallmark of the women's campaign. The Women's Heney Club gathered at the League headquarters every Thursday afternoon, as the Branch had done in the past. In addition, the CLJ's organ, The Liberator, announced meetings at the homes of supporters. It reported on September 25, "All of the home meetings have been largely attended. The speakers on all occasions brought home to their hearers the fact that the issue of the campaign for district attorney is primarily a moral issue and that the contest is not between individuals, but is a struggle for a principle."[63]

Heney Club leaders drew in other women's organizations. The Club presented its case before the California Equal Suffrage Association in late September. On October 1, CESA Central Committee Chair Lillian Harris Coffin enthusiastically endorsed Heney, commenting, "We are for Heney and are organizing in every district of the city." On October 12, the Woman's Christian Temperance League added its endorsement to the list.[64]

However, politics triumphed over principle and Heney's opponent, Charles Fickert, easily won the race. Fickert's platform included a pledge to end the graft prosecution if elected, and Fickert followed through with his promise. Soon afterward, the League disbanded.[65]

San Francisco club women had an additional reason to shift their attention away from the League with the national increase in woman suffrage activity. In 1910, Washington state passed a measure granting woman suffrage. Even prior to that, California woman suffrage clubs had regrouped in order to commence the ultimately victorious 1911 campaign. Elizabeth Gerberding became president of the Woman Suffrage Party. Lillian H. Coffin and Mary Sperry returned to the CESA to continue their tenure as vice president and president. Coffin also founded the Club Woman's Franchise League in 1911. Alice Park headed up the massive literature campaign for the CESA during the 1911 effort. Franchesca Pierce, a Woman's Branch "district chairman," continued as CESA corresponding secretary. Member Mary Gamage became president of the San Francisco Equal Suffrage League and treasurer of the CESA. Presumably, these women also returned to their club work, if they had ever left it.[66]

Women's Branch activists in the CLJ also applied their acquired political skills during the 1911 California woman suffrage campaign. The Woman Suffrage Party, led by Gerberding, mobilized feminists on the level of city precincts. Its organizational structure resembled that of the Woman's Branch and its "District Chairmen."[67]

The suffrage movement and women's anti-graft organizations overlapped considerably from 1908-1910. The identification of leading suffragists with pro-prosecution forces was clear and unequivocal, one which union women would come to view with scorn and contempt.

When word of the Board of Supervisors graft confessions hit the papers in March 1907, labor's response was immediate. The <u>Labor Clarion</u> demanded that the Board of Supervisors, mostly composed of ULP members, either prove its innocence or resign. The <u>Clarion</u> article complained that workingmen elected the Board in 1905 in good faith and that their trust had been violated. The following week, the San Francisco Labor Council announced in the <u>Labor Clarion</u> its belief that <u>all</u> wrongdoers should be prosecuted and disassociated itself from those charged with graft. The <u>Coast Seamen's Journal</u> railed against the betrayal of the ULP administration, dubbing it "a crime against union hopes."[68]

Ruef's trial began on May 15, 1907, barely a week after the start of the streetcar strike. While the strike received far more coverage than the graft trials, labor papers still found space to comment on the graft prosecution and its consequences for the labor community. By early summer, the <u>Labor Clarion</u> ran an article holding the prosecution responsible for the chaotic state of San Francisco's municipal government and blaming it for the nonresolution of the streetcar and telephone strikes. The article implied that the prosecution was more interested in usurping power than guaranteeing capable and honest city government.[69]

During the summer of 1907, three factions vied for power in the ULP. When the smoke had cleared, Building Trades Council President P.H. McCarthy emerged as the victor in the party's August primary by touting an anti-prosecution stance with McCarthy as the mayoral candidate. In the general elections campaign, however, McCarthy downplayed this position, sensing rightly that the pro-reform atmosphere would not tolerate criticism of the trials. Louise

LaRue reported that Waitresses Local 48 members supported McCarthy by riding in cars bearing his campaign banners in the Labor Day parade. Labor, however, split ranks over McCarthy's candidacy and the ULP ticket went down to defeat. Michael Kazin identified the cause of the rift as "a combination of antagonism towards McCarthy and reluctance to oppose the popular warriors of reform".[70]

By the time of the next election in 1909, the San Francisco public had grown war-weary of the seemingly never-ending trials, which had failed to convict anyone except Ruef but which nevertheless continued. By then, the rupture within the ULP of two years before was forgotten and labor united around mayoral candidate McCarthy. This time, LaRue and Local 48 backed a winning team. McCarthy won by exploiting growing frustration with the graft prosecution and appealing to workers.[71]

Aside from supporting McCarthy, women unionists' support for the anti-prosecution forces took another form during the 1909 campaign. At the same time the Women's Heney Club began promoting Heney, The Liberator produced an article from the San Francisco Evening Post reporting that Mrs. E.H. (Minna) O'Donnell, a leader of the Wage Earner's Suffrage League and of the Woman's Auxiliary #18 of International Typographical Union Local 21 in San Francisco, helped form the Women's Municipal League (WML). The WML sought to end the graft prosecution and propagandized that the money spent on it would be more wisely spent bettering the school system, improving the streets, and acquiring more land for parks and playgrounds. Reformers certainly did not miss the sarcasm of these demands, which snidely parroted measures usually put forth by them.[72]

Despite the deepening wedge between themselves and reform suffragists, the unionists continued to identify themselves as suffragists and to work actively for the women's franchise. In August 1908, LaRue attended the Republican state convention in Oakland as part of a three-person delegation from Local 48. The delegation, along with over one hundred other suffragists, descended on the convention with signs and banners, demanding that the Republicans adopt a woman suffrage plank to the party platform. The resolution failed. Undaunted, the Local 48 delegation announced that they planned to travel on to Stockton the next week to lobby for a similar plank in the Democratic Party platform. The Democrats had endorsed votes for women at their previous convention and reiterated their support. The Labor Clarion faithfully recorded each attempt and identified Local 48 as being "active in the suffrage agitation."[73]

In 1909, the San Francisco Labor Council and the San Francisco Building Trades Council sponsored Louise LaRue as a delegate to the National Women's Trade Union League Convention in Chicago.[74] At the convention, LaRue reported on the split between the two groups of suffragists. After recalling the blow-up between reform and union suffragists, LaRue claimed that the unionists tried to maintain an outward appearance of friendliness towards the Equal Suffrage League to prevent anti-suffrage forces from making hay out of the schism. "We felt that we did not get on together--that the working women and women like that cannot mix, and the only thing to do is to separate and try to be as pleasant as we can and let outsiders think we are harmonious," she explained.[75]

By the time LaRue attended the NWTUL Convention, she and other union suffragists had taken concrete steps to assure that labor would maintain a presence in the suffrage campaign. They founded the Wage Earners Suffrage League (WESL) on September 22, 1908. The WESL pledged to advocate and win "better conditions for working women and . . . to promote the suffrage idea." Founding members chose Louise LaRue as their secretary and Mrs. Will French, wife of the Labor Clarion's editor, as treasurer. Minna O'Donnell became the organization's president. O'Donnell announced the news of the WESL's birth in her column in the Labor Clarion, "Women's Department," which she had initiated one month earlier.[76]

Two weeks after the WESL held its founding meeting, Minna O'Donnell appeared before the San Francisco Equal Suffrage League at their invitation. According to a report in the San Francisco Call, the reform suffragists hoped to effect a reunion with their sisters across the class divide. During her speech, O'Donnell took the opportunity to remind the reform suffragists of the issues and conditions which differentiated them from the WESL. "It has been suggested that our league join hands with yours," O'Donnell began, "but that is out of the question. . . We can not join you and we can not send representatives to your gatherings. . . We want the ballot for very different reasons from the ones you have for wanting it. Our idea is self-protection; you want it to use for some one else."[77] O'Donnell was apparently referring to the reform suffragists' stated intention to pursue the goals of progressivism, such as political reform, slum elimination, and temperance, versus the union suffragists intent to work for legislation that would directly benefit the women and men of their own class.

Maud Younger, a WESL activist, backed up O'Donnell's point, adding, "(Woman suffrage is) just a question of sex with the women of the league, but with us - and I am a union woman myself - it is a question of the things that affect men and women alike." Younger further noted that unions had remained aloof from the suffrage movement because they suspected that reform suffragists were "using the unions as tools only," and were not interested in labor's aims. Other WESL activists present agreed, charging that the Equal Suffrage League only wanted the strength and influence of the WESL's working-class membership; a point the reform suffragists adamantly denied. The meeting broke up before the reformers made any progress towards reconciliation.[78]

Despite their differences with the reformers and their unyielding position on a separate body, the WESL activists maintained the appearance of solidarity with the Equal Suffrage League. LaRue told the NWTUL convention that she and other unionists traveled to Sacramento in 1909 to speak on behalf of the woman suffrage bill submitted to the state legislature. "We went to the legislature and backed their bill," LaRue said pointedly. John I. Nolan legislative agent for the California Federation of Labor, accompanied the hopeful delegation to lobby for woman suffrage. Introduced again by Assembly Representative Grove Johnson, the bill was narrowly defeated in the Assembly by a vote of 39-37.[79]

Union suffragists and their reform-minded sisters attempted and failed to merge their energies and resources in a single organization in the effort to win woman suffrage. Unlike feminists in New York, Boston, and Chicago with a brief history of cross-class alliance in organizations such as the Women's Trade Union League, San Francisco reform suffragists had little experience working with women from a background and culture different from their own. This first effort, apparently initiated by women unionists who were pro-suffrage, proved to be extremely brittle. Pre-existing differences between union and reform suffragists on the desirability of union organizing over legislation and on the use of alcohol, compounded by divergent views on the graft trials and Union Labor Party undermined whatever chance the alliance had for survival. The 1907 streetcar strike dealt the final blow to their working relationship within the San Francisco Equal Suffrage League.

While middle-class suffragists promoted the notion of the commonality of all women and social harmony, other women recognized that merely wishing it would not make it so. Speaking at a 1910 socialist women's conference to discuss working within mainstream suffrage organizations, May Wood Simons warned that suffragists "cannot wipe away class struggle among women and say it is just a beautiful sisterhood." In her role as an organizer for the International Workers of the World, Elizabeth Gurley Flynn echoed this conviction in an article in the IWW journal Solidarity. Calling the notion of sisterhood "a hollow sham to labor," she causticly disabused her readers of the possibility of an alliance with middle-class feminists. Behind the facade of unity lurked "smug hypocrisy and sickly sentimentality." Flynn maintained that the only gender allies that working-class women had were themselves. Following the split, women such as LaRue probably would have agreed.[80]

Class and cultural disparity stood at the heart of this schism. While woman suffrage, and indeed gender status, provided an issue these two groups of women could rally around, each group adhered to a separate constellation of values that was often the antithesis of the other's beliefs. These divergences repeatedly polarized them and foiled their attempts to work in concert with one another.

As the WESL, union women continued to support the efforts of the mainstream suffrage organization but as a separate group. They sought the support of the labor community and participated in actions directed towards influencing the Democratic and Republican parties as well as the state legislature. Though disillusioned by the uncomradely reaction of the Equal Suffrage League to the streetcar boycott, they remained committed to the suffrage cause and to the notion that the vote, in combination with the more powerful force of collective bargaining, was a significant means of improving working conditions for women. However, the WESL and their reformist counterparts would have to wait until the 1911 legislative session to raise the question again.

NOTES TO CHAPTER TWO

1.   Mary McHenry Keith, "California in 1901-1920," Keith-McHenry-Pond Papers, carton 3, File "Woman Suffrage Campaign in California," Bancroft Library, University of California, Berkeley, California; Donald Waller Rodes, "The California Woman Suffrage Campaign of 1911" (M.A. thesis, California State University, Hayward, 1974), 7-10, 23-25.

2.   Eleanor Flexner, <u>Century of Struggle</u> (Cambridge: Belknap Press, 1959; New York: Atheneum, 1973), 248-249. The movement had experienced a dry period before. Over twenty years passed between the time that Wyoming and Utah legislated women's right to the ballot, respectively in 1869 and 1870, and Colorado's male voters voted to grant women suffrage in 1893. During this time, the woman suffrage movement split into two opposing groups over the inclusion of sex as well race as criteria for the due process of citizenship and the right to vote in the Fourteenth and Fifteenth Amendments to the United States Constitution. The rift healed in 1890 with the merger of the two groups into the National American Woman Suffrage Association, an amalgamation of both groups' names. Flexner, <u>Century of Struggle</u>, 142-155, 164-178, 216-220. See also Ellen Carol DuBois, <u>Feminism and Suffrage</u> (Ithaca: Cornell University Press, 1978), 52-202.

3.   Rodes, "The California Woman Suffrage Campaign of 1911," 8; Arthur S. Link and Richard L. McCormick, <u>Progressivism</u> (Arlington Heights, Ill.: Harlan Davidson, Inc.,1983), 102-103; Prohibitionists relied on a legal tactic called the local option to reduce liquor sales in California. Local option laws permitted each community or county to vote on whether or not liquor would be sold within its borders. See Gilman M. Ostrander, <u>The Prohibition Movement in California, 1848-1933</u>, University of California Publications in History, vol. 57 (Berkeley and Los Angeles: University of California Press, 1957).

4.   Flexner, <u>Century of Struggle</u>, 183-185; Ruth Bordin, <u>Frances Willard</u> (Chapel Hill: University of North Carolina Press, 1986), 79-102.

5.   Ostrander, <u>The Prohibition Movement in California, 1848-1933</u>, 44-54, 53.   The Women's Crusade was a national phenomenon. Beginning in December of 1873, the Crusade fanned out from its starting point in Ohio and sparked prohibition movements in a number of states through 1874. Ohio and the midwestern region, however, remained the area of most intense activity. During the Crusade, an estimated 25,000 saloons closed their doors in the face of the women's preachments. The results did not appear to be lasting as most of the saloons and other establishments reopened after six to eight months,

however, the women prohibitionists founded the WCTU in November 1874. Herbert Asbury, The Great Illusion: An Informal History of Prohibition (New York: Doubleday, 1950), 68-87; Ruth Bordin, Woman and Temperance: The Quest for Power and Liberty, 1873-1900 (Philadelphia: Temple University Press, 1981),15-51.

6.   Ostrander, The Prohibition Movement in California, 1848-1933, 53; Eleanor Flexner, Century of Struggle, 185. Ruth Bordin characterized the relationship between the National American Woman Suffrage Association (NAWSA) and the WCTU in the late nineteenth century as mutually supportive but uneasy. NAWSA leaders Anna Howard Shaw and Mary Livermore also participated visibly in WCTU campaigns. Susan B. Anthony and Frances Willard maintained a lifelong friendship and their correspondence documented each other's activities. Yet, WCTU activists in the 1896 California woman suffrage campaign were asked to "remove their white ribbons and remain silent on prohibition," demands they considered "an indignity." In 1899, NAWSA President Carrie Chapman Catt advised the WCTU to relinquish all suffrage agitation to NAWSA, a proposal the temperance women strongly rejected. Bordin, Woman and Temperance, 121-122. The California WCTU experienced its heyday from the mid-1870s until 1898, when the largely male Anti-Saloon League established a California branch of the organization. The League asserted itself as the main temperance organization in the state and the WCTU followed its lead for the rest of the campaign for prohibition. Ironically, the League was initially formed to provide support for the Women's Crusade in 1874. Ostrander, The Prohibition Movement in California, 1848-1933, 60-85; Asbury, The Great Illusion, 94-96.

7.   Reda Davis, California Women: A Guide to Their Politics, 1885-1911 (San Francisco: no publisher, 1967), 78; Rodes, "The California Woman Suffrage Campaign of 1911", 8; Keith, "California in 1901-1920".

8.   Laughlin travelled extensively on behalf of the cause for woman suffrage. She eventually returned to San Francisco in 1914 to set up a law office and became active in state Republican politics. She joined the National Women's Party at the same time as Maud Younger, who would figure prominently in the future of the Wage Earners' Suffrage League. Barbara Sicherman, and others, Notable American Women: The Modern Period (Cambridge: Belknap Press, 1980), 410-411.

9.   Keith, "California in 1901-1920."

10.   Rodes, "The California Woman Suffrage Campaign of 1911," 27-28; Selina Solomons, How We Won the Vote in California: A True Story of the Campaign of 1911 (San Francisco: the New Woman Publishing Co., n.d.), 4.

11.   San Francisco Chronicle, 28 August 1949; San Francisco Bulletin 23 January 1909; 14 April 1909; 1 September 1908.

12.   Solomons, How We Won The Vote, 4.

13.   Founded in 1888, the Century Club was a bastion of San Francisco high society women such as Phoebe Hearst, the club's first president, and Mrs. Benjamin Ide Wheeler, wife of the president of the University of California, Berkeley. Like the California Club, it was affiliated with the General Federation of Women's Clubs. California Federation of Women's Clubs, Who's Who Among the Women of California (San Francisco and Los Angeles: Security Publishing Co., 1922), 93, 252; Karen J. Blair, The Clubwoman as Feminist: True Womanhood Redefined, 1868-1914 (New York: Holmes & Meier Pub., Inc., 1980), 37, 95; Century Club, First Report of the Century Club (San Francisco: Crocker & Co., 1898), 24.

14.   Rodes, "The California Woman Suffrage Campaign of 1911," 28-29; Keith, "California in 1901-1920", California Federation of Women's Clubs, Club Women of California (San Francisco: California Federation of Women's Clubs, 1907-08), 17-23, 45-47. Sargent's husband, U.S. Senator Aron A. Sargent, first introduced the "Anthony Amendment" in 1878. Congress eventually passed this same bill in 1919 as the Nineteenth Amendment to the U.S. Constitution. The states ratified the "Anthony Amendment," granting enfranchisement to women, in 1920. Flexner, Century of Struggle, 173.

15.   Keith, "California in 1901-1920." While clubwomen represented a significant proportion of the CESA leadership, as well as that of local suffrage organizations in San Francisco, the California Federation of Women's Clubs did not endorse woman suffrage until 1911. However, individual clubs such as the California Club took positions earlier. In 1908, the CESA State Convention was held at the California Club. Rodes, "The California Woman Suffrage Campaign of 1911," 27-28; Keith, "California in 1901-1920".

16.   Karen J. Blair, The Clubwoman as Feminist (New York: Holmes & Meier Pub., Inc., 1980), 93-119.

17.   Robert Wiebe, The Search For Order, 1877-1920 (New York: Hill and Wang, 1967). Wiebe concentrated mainly on traditional political aspects of Progressivism and reserved little space for the spheres of activity which involved women such as suffrage, temperance, settlement house work, and other movements characterized by the labels social justice and social control. Works which remedy this flaw include Arthur S. Link and Richard L. McCormick, Progressivism (Arlington Heights, Ill.: Harlan Davidson, Inc., 1983), 67-104; Linda K. Kerber and Jane DeHart-Mathews, Women's America (New York and

Oxford: Oxford University Press, 1982), 221-322; Sheila M. Rothman, Woman's
Proper Place (New York: Basic Books, Inc., 1978); Blair, The Clubwoman as
Feminist; and Eleanor Flexner, Century of Struggle, 203-215.

18.   "Proceedings of 1909 Convention," September 29, p. 24, National
Women's Trade Union League Papers (henceforth NWTUL), Microfilm, Reel
19, Library of Congress, Washington, D.C.

19.   Rodes, "The California Woman Suffrage Campaign of 1911," 36. Grove
Johnson was Hiram Johnson's father.   Hiram would not share his father's
enthusiasm for woman suffrage.

20.   San Francisco Examiner, 3 September 1911.

21.   Examiner, 28 February 1908.

22.   San Francisco Call, 22 July 1909; Chronicle, 22 July 1909; Examiner,
22 July 1909.

23.   Jon M. Kingsdale, "The 'Poor Man's Club': Social Functions of the
Urban Working-Class Saloon," American Quarterly 25 (October 1973): 472-489.

24.   Kingsdale, "'Poor Man's Club'", 482; Call, 27 February 1908; Labor
Clarion, 5 March 1909. While unions did decry excess drinking, working-class
and immigrant communities preferred to look to internal institutions to remedy
the situation. The Labor Clarion of May 28, 1909, reported on labor temperance
fellowships in Europe, perhaps in the hope that it would stimulate such
organizations in the United States. The San Francisco Italian community had one
such temperance organization called the League of the Cross Cadets; The
Monitor, 20 May 1911. Elements of San Francisco's Irish community founded
temperance groups during the nineteenth century, however the organizations
failed to survive. Burchell commented that this was partially due to the Catholic
Church's indifference to temperance. While the temperance groups usually met
in churches, parish priests typically remained uninvolved and the groups died of
disinterest from both clergy and the community at large. Robert A. Burchell,
The San Francisco Irish, 1848-1880 (Manchester, Great Britain: Manchester
University Press, 1979), 105-106. It should also be noted that temperance and
prohibition were generally neglected issues in northern California.   The
California Anti-Saloon League's Northern Division passed out of existence during
this period due to "lack of popular support."   Ostrander, The Prohibition
Movement in California, 1848-1933, 64.

25.   Alice Kessler-Harris, "Where Are the Organized Women Workers?" in

Kerber and DeHart-Mathews, Women's America, 244; Labor Clarion, passim., 1907-1911.

26.   Mary Jones, The Autobiography of Mother Jones (Chicago: Charles Kerr & Co., 1972), 239; Dale Fetherling, Mother Jones, The Miner's Angel: A Portrait (Carbondale: Southern Illinois University Press, 1974), 166.

27.   Lucille Eaves, A History of California Labor Legislation with an Introductory Sketch of the San Francisco Labor Movement, vol. 2 (Berkeley: University of California Press, 1910), 313; Joan M. Jensen and Gloria R. Lothrup, California Women: A History (San Francisco: Boyd and Fraser Publishing Co., 1987), 58; Mixer and Server, 20 (April 1911): 16; Dorothy Sue Cobble, "'Practical Women': Waitress Unionists and the Controversies Over Gender Roles in the Food Service Industry, 1900-1980," Labor History 29 (Winter 1988): 15-23. Interestingly, LaRue reported that Waiters' Local 17 in Los Angeles supported a local ordinance which barred women from serving or selling liquor. This denied waitresses there the ability to work in several "good houses." While this may point up regional forces at work, LaRue contended that the Los Angeles union waiters favored the law because it was "good for the boys." LaRue charged the Los Angeles local with displacing women from lucrative restaurants. Whether the waiters intentionally sought to eliminate women from higher-paying jobs or bent to the prohibitionist climate of Los Angeles is unclear. There was, however, no mistaking the antagonism expressed by their sister local from San Francisco. Mixer and Server, 20 (April 1911): 16. Cobble described the distrust most waitresses felt towards middle-class women because of their crusades for prohibition and red light abatement; Dorothy Sue Cobble, "Sisters in the Craft: Waitresses and Their Unions in the Twentieth Century," 2 vols. (Ph D. dissertation, Stanford University, 1986), 151-152.

28.   Lillian Matthews, Women in Trade Unions in San Francisco, University of California Publications in Economics, vol.3 (Berkeley: University of California, 1913), 81; Cobble, "Sisters in the Craft," 312, 151-153; Louise Ploeger, "Trade Unionism Among the Women of San Francisco 1920" (M.A. thesis, University of California, Berkeley, 1920), 122.

29.   Ida Husted Harper, Life and Work of Susan B. Anthony, 3 vols. (New York: Arno Press, 1969), 1162.

30.   Coast Seaman's Journal, 2 April 1913; Matthews, Women in the Trade Unions in San Francisco, 92; Ploeger, "Trade Unionism Among the Women of San Francisco 1920," 130-131.

31.   Robert Edward Lee Knight, Industrial Relations in the San Francisco Bay Area, 1900-1918 (Berkeley and Los Angeles: University of California Press, 1960), 186; Chronicle, 5 May 1907.

32.   Chronicle, 6 May 1907; Examiner, 6 May 1907.

33.   Knight, Industrial Relations in the San Francisco Bay Area, 187.

34.   Labor Clarion, 10 May 1907; Knight, Industrial Relations in the San Francisco Bay Area, 187-88; Chronicle, 8 May 1907; Examiner, 8 May 1907. Because Mayor Eugene Schmitz represented the Union Labor Party, no city police guarded the United Railroad cars. As a matter of fact, Schmitz publicly announced that the police would not be used to protect strikebreakers. Examiner, 7 May 1907.

35.   Examiner, 8 May 1907; Chronicle, 8 May 1907; Knight, Industrial Relations in the San Francisco Bay Area, 188.

36.   Knight, Industrial Relations in the San Francisco Bay Area, 186-188; Examiner, 8 May 1907; Chronicle, 8 May 1907. William Issel and Robert W. Cherny, San Francisco 1865-1932 (Berkeley and Los Angeles: University of California Press, 1986), 19-21.

37.   Knight, Industrial Relations in the San Francisco Bay Area, 18; Labor Clarion, 17 May 1907; Chronicle, 8 May 1907.

38.   Labor Clarion, 26 July 1907.

39.   Knight, Industrial Relations in the San Francisco Bay Area, 193-197.

40.   Knight, Industrial Relations in the San Francisco Bay Area, 193-197; Labor Clarion, 13 September 1907.

41.   Chronicle, 9 May 1907; Chronicle, 10 May 1907; Examiner, 10 May 1907; 11 May 1907.

42.   Chronicle, 12 May 1907; Examiner, 12 May 1907. It should be noted that the Examiner's coverage of women passengers did not appear until page 32, in contrast to the Chronicle's page 2 reportage. The strike itself, however, continued to command a front-page spot in the Examiner.

43.   Examiner, 12 May 1907. In early May, 1907, approximately 500 women telephone operators employed by Pacific Telephone and Telegraph Company went on strike to demand union recognition and decent wages, and to protest the firing of union members. Lillian Mathews reported that, at the time of the

strike, ten to twenty percent of operators were members of the fledgling Telephone Operators Union. The San Francisco Labor Council initially solicited funds to support the strike and endorsed a sympathy strike staged by the Electrical Linemen's Union. The telephone operators ended their strike three months later when the Labor Council told the union's leaders that the company agreed to increase wages and rehire the strikers. Despite these reassurances, P.T. and T. refused to reinstate the many Telephone Operators Union members. Drained of its activists, the union eventually dissolved. Labor Clarion, 3, 10 and 31 May 1907; Matthews, Women in the Trade Unions of San Francisco, 87; Knight, Industrial Relations in the San Francisco Bay Area, 186, 191-192.

44.   Examiner, 14 May 1907; Chronicle, 14 May 1907.

45.   Labor Clarion, 24 May 1907, 2 August 1907; Knight, Industrial Relations in the San Francisco Bay Area, 196; Labor Clarion, 14 June 1907. The strike fund was a combined effort of the San Francisco Labor Council and the Building Trades Council. Call, 8 May 1907; Labor Clarion, 10 May 1907.

46.   "Proceedings of 1909 Convention," NWTUL Papers, September 29, p. 26.

47.   "Proceedings of 1909 Convention," NWTUL Papers, September 29, p. 26.

48.   For a full account of the Great Uprising of the garment workers, see Meredith Tax, The Rising of the Women (New York: Monthly Review Press, 1980) and Barbara M. Wertheimer, We Were There (New York: Pantheon Books, 1977), 293-317. Nancy Schrom Dye described the strike from the Women's Trade Union League's perspective in As Equals and As Sisters (Columbia, Mo.: University of Missouri Press, 1980), 88-109.

49.   "Proceedings of 1909 Convention," NWTUL papers, September 29, p. 26.

50.   Issel and Cherny, San Francisco 1865-1932, 66-68, 78. Women who were truly wealthy presumably had private transportation at their disposal and could afford to denounce the strike on principle. They were also more likely to travel in the social circles frequented by those such as Calhoun and other corporate officials. Suffragist Mary McHenry Keith's husband was good friends with William Herrin, attorney for the Southern Pacific Railroad. Keith-McHenry-Pond papers, Box 2, file "William Herrin".

51.   Issel and Cherny, San Francisco 1865-1932, 58-66.

52.   Jules Tygiel, "'Where Unionism Holds Undisputed Sway' -- A Reappraisal of San Francisco's Union Labor Party," California History 62 (Fall 1983): 196-215; Walton Bean, Boss Ruef's San Francisco (Berkeley and Los Angeles, University of California Press, 1968). Both sources chronicle the emergence and development of the Union Labor Party. Tygiel demonstrated that working-class voters provided the ULP with its primary base of support and that it was entitled to call itself a labor party. Bean's book focuses on the graft trials.

53.   Bean, Boss Ruef's San Francisco, 188-197; Examiner, 12 July 1908.

54.   Bean, Boss Ruef's San Francisco, 188-197.

55.   Bean, Boss Ruef's San Francisco, 256-267; The Liberator, 12 December 1908; Bulletin, 22 June 1908.

56.   Minutes, Woman's Branch meeting, 17 September 1908, Citizen's League for Justice Papers (henceforth CLJ), Box 103, Franklin Hichborn Collection, University Research Library, University of California, Los Angeles; Bulletin, 27 October 1909. Elizabeth Gerberding, "Women Fight Against Graft in San Francisco," Delineator 76 (October 1910): 245-246, 322-323 recounts Gerberding's activity in the CLJ.

57.   Elizabeth Gerberding to George Boke, 1 September 1909, CLJ papers, Box 103; "District Chairmen," CLJ papers, Box 103; Lillian Harris Coffin to the CLJ, 17 June 1909, CLJ papers, Box 103; Bulletin, 16 March 1909; The Liberator, 15 September 1909; California Federation of Women's Clubs, Club Women, 37; Bulletin, 28 November 1908; California Federation of Women's Clubs, Club Women 57, 17-23, 45-47; Bulletin, 24 April, 1909. According to the San Francisco Call, Coffin and Gamage had unsuccessfully tried to launch a similar group in March, 1908. Coffin called for a "women's campaign against graft" that would involve all women. She made a special plea to union women to join. Coffin pledged to "lend aid to Langdon (the district attorney) and Heney." The group was to meet in April of 1908. Apparently Coffin's effort did not get off the ground because nothing further was mentioned about a women's anti-graft organization until the Women's Branch took its place. Call, 21 March 1908.

58.   CLJ recruitment letter, 28 August 1908, CLJ papers, Box 103; CLJ recruitment letter, 16 September 1908, CLJ papers, Box 103; Elizabeth Gerberding, "Women Fight Against Graft in San Francisco," Delineator 76 (October 1910): 245; CLJ papers, see Box 103, File "1908-1909 Correspondence"; Gerberding, "Women Fight," 245.

59.   The Liberator, 16 January 1909; Gerberding, "Women Fight," 245.

60.   The Liberator, 16 January 1909; Bulletin, 16 March 1909; 19 April 1909; The Liberator, 16 January 1909.

61.   Keith, "California in 1901-1920".

62.   The Liberator, 24 July 1909; Bulletin, 12 June, 24 August, 31 August 1909.

63.   Gerberding, "Women Fight," 322; The Liberator, 25 September 1909, 9 October 1909. Novelist Miriam Michelson came up with the idea to initiate The Liberator and acted as the associate publisher for December 1908 and January 1909.   Although her name disappeared from the masthead after that time, she continued to contribute articles and essays. The Liberator, 12 December 1908-23 January 1909; 6 February 1909. She later spoke out for woman suffrage, touting it as a way to end "social evil." Call, 1 July 1911; Miriam Michelson, "Vice and the Women's Vote," Sunset Magazine (April 1913): 345-348.

64.   The Liberator, 2 October 1909; Bulletin, 1 October, 12 October 1909

65.   Bean, Boss Ruef's San Francisco, 299. The Liberator, 15 January, 22 January 1910; also CLJ papers Box 104.

66.   Solomons, How We Won the Vote, 25; Schrom Dye, As Equals and As Sisters, 130; Solomons, How We Won the Vote, 24-25; Mary McHenry Keith, "California in 1901-1920."

67.   Schrom Dye, As Equals and As Sisters, 130; The Liberator, 26 December 1908; 16 January 1909.

68.   Labor Clarion, 22 March, 29 March 1907; Coast Seaman's Journal, 27 March 1907.

69.   Labor Clarion, 12 July 1907. Labor did not unanimously oppose the prosecution. Three notable exceptions were Andrew Furuseth, president of the Sailors Union of the Pacific, Michael Casey, the Teamster Union's chief, and Carmen president Richard Cornelius, all of whom backed the prosecution. Furuseth and Casey feared that the scandal would taint the entire labor movement. While Cornelius claimed to have the same motivation, it is clear that he viewed the trials as a way to strike back at Patrick Calhoun, United Railroad president and a defendant in the graft trials. Michael Kazin, Barons of Labor: The San Francisco Building Trades and Union Power in the Progressive Era (Urbana and Chicago: University of Illinois Press, 1986) 131-132, 137-139.

70.   Kazin, Barons of Labor, 136-139; "Proceedings of 1909 Convention," NWTUL Papers, September 29, pp. 21-22; Kazin, "Barons of Labor: The San Francisco Building Trades, 1896-1920" (Ph.D. dissertation, Stanford University, 1983), 298.

71.   Bean, Boss Ruef's San Francisco, 264-267.

72.   The Liberator, 11 September 1909; San Francisco Evening Post, 4 September 1909.

73.   Labor Clarion, 1 May, 10 July, 28 August 1908; Rodes, "The California Woman Suffrage Campaign of 1911," 38-39; Labor Clarion, 28 August 1908.

74.   Building Trades Council to San Francisco Labor Council, 3 September 1909, file "Building Trades Council," Box 3, San Francisco Labor Council Papers, Bancroft Library, University of California, Berkeley, California; Labor Clarion, 13 August, 3 September, 17 September, 1909.

75.   "Proceedings of the 1909 Convention," NWTUL Papers, September 29, p. 26.

76.   Labor Clarion, 25 September 1908.

77.   Call, 4 October 1908.

78.   Call, 4 October 1908.

79.   "Proceedings of the 1909 Convention," NWTUL Papers, September 29, p.27; Labor Clarion, 8 January, 22 January 1909; Rodes, "The California Woman Suffrage Campaign of 1911," 39.

80.   Bruce Dancis, "Socialism and Women in the United States, 1900-1917," Socialist Revolution 6 (January-March 1976): 119; Tax, The Rising of the Women, 12.

CHAPTER 3

"TO SECURE THE LABOR VOTE":
UNION WOMEN AND THE "LAST PUSH" FOR WOMAN SUFFRAGE IN
CALIFORNIA

Shortly after the triumphant 1911 campaign for woman suffrage in
California, veteran suffragist Selina Solomons composed a memoir of the final
years of the quest for enfranchisement. The account, How We Won the Vote in
California: A True Story of the Campaign of 1911, was a joyous vindication of
the belief that Californians could be convinced that women deserved full
citizenship rights. In Solomons's view, the instigation of the San Francisco graft
trials in October 1906 marked the beginning of the "last push" to win the ballot
for women.[1]

1906 was indeed an eventful year for the California suffrage movement.
Lillian Harris Coffin's disillusionment with the California Club and the founding
of the San Francisco Equal Suffrage League in 1906 helped bring fresh blood and
organizational coherence to the suffrage movement in San Francisco. The
Northern California movement survived administrative disaster when the
earthquake of 1906 destroyed "much valuable suffrage data." Undaunted, the
California Equal Suffrage Association's board of officers met one month later to
commit themselves to adding woman suffrage as a plank in the political platforms
of the state Democratic and Republican parties. California suffragists like Mary
Sperry travelled to Oregon to assist their compatriots in the Northwest in an

unsuccessful campaign for enfranchisement. The California Equal Suffrage Association pledged $1000 towards Oregon's quest for the vote.[2]

It was also in 1906 that the Union Labor Party of San Francisco first endorsed woman suffrage and the demand became a plank in the ULP platform. Ida Husted Harper, who assumed the task of documenting the final decades of the suffrage struggle, noted that a Miss Maud Younger aided the Legislative Committee of the CESA in obtaining this significant endorsement.[3]

Maud Younger proved to be the keystone that supported the relationship between the labor and suffrage movements in San Francisco and, perhaps, all of California. Born in San Francisco of upper middle-class parents in 1870, Younger and her siblings inherited a "substantial fortune" at age twelve upon their mother's death. In her early years, Younger led a life suitable to that of the child of a prominent dentist. She grew into a young debutante, filling her time with an active social and church life and voyages abroad.[4]

Younger's life was transformed from that of a socialite to one of activism on one such journey. In 1901, she set out from San Francisco to visit her father in Paris. He had settled there one year earlier and established a practice as a dentist of high society. During her stay in New York before the voyage, Younger visited the College Settlement in the city's Lower East Side. Graduates of Smith, Wellesley, Vassar, Bryn Mawr, and Radcliffe (then known as Harvard Annex) founded the Settlement in 1889 to attack the social problems resulting from urbanization and industrialization. Younger, curious to learn about the condition of life in the surrounding tenements, asked to stay "for a few days."[5]

Younger did not leave New York until five years later. The experience of wading knee-deep into the world of over-crowded and dank housing, grueling sweatshop labor, and "the evils undermining the moral and physical health of women, . . . too tired to resist the onslaughts of disease and crime" irresistibly attracted Younger and molded her into an advocate of the working-class, particularly women. It eventually convinced Younger that the settlement movement "was not the whole answer to the woes of the poor," according to friend and fellow suffrage activist Inez Haynes Irwin. Younger resented the patronizing superiority of settlement house workers towards their working-class clients. In her autobiography, Younger remembered with regret ". . . the artificial relation between settlement worker and the neighborhood. For however warm the friendships, we were there as a favored class on a basis of superiority, to help those less fortunate. . . . The only true bond is not where one is in a superior position, but where both work together for some common end, for civic betterment, community projects, in some movement such as labor, suffrage, even political parties. . . " She turned her back on the types of social reform favored by settlement house workers and became a convert to union organizing. "A trade unionist--of course I am," Younger would later proclaim, "First, last and all the time."[6]

Younger described her conversion in an article she wrote for McClure's Magazine documenting an investigation of the working conditions of women restaurant workers. Younger spent one summer in New York working at various restaurants for firsthand experience. Her journal entries detailed the difficulties in finding a job (especially when one had no experience), the exhaustion and hunger from being on one's feet for hours without a break, and the innumerable excuses employers used to extract fines from the waitresses.[7]

"You're fined if you break anything; you're fined if the ice melts on the butter so that the water runs on the table; you're fined if the spoon ain't in the sugar bowl. There's mighty few girls that get full wages here. The firm sometimes makes a dollar a week off a girl," confided one of Younger's coworkers. Another waitress confirmed Younger's suspicion that most of the women could not support themselves on their wages and supplemented their wages by finding "some other means of support." Often, male customers supplied that means, trading dates with the "girls" for money and clothing. Younger intimated that sexual favors were also a part of the bargain.[8]

Such conversations among the waitresses sometimes drifted to talk of unions and organizing. Younger shied away from being drawn into such discussions initially, expressing shock that some of her fellow waitresses had participated in a strike two years before.[9] By the time she worked at a branch of Childs' restaurant, however, Younger's disposition towards unions had changed. She worked with union agitator Katie Martin, who rotated workplaces frequently in order to be able to "talk unions" with her constituency. Martin urged her to join the union. Although Younger had no intention of continuing as a waitress, she obtained her union card. At the end of the article, Younger gushed, "I want to be a walking delegate like Katie!"[10]

Younger joined the New York chapter of the National Women's Trade Union League (NWTUL) in December 1904, becoming an executive board member soon after. She lived in a tenement apartment across the street from the group's local headquarters. As chair of the Waitresses' Committee, she helped organize the New York Waitresses' Union, an independent waitresses' local and argued that the NYWTUL should make organizing waitresses an organizational priority. The New York WTUL's masthead listed Younger as a representative of that union. Reminiscing about the many different hats she wore in the organization, Younger called herself "a maid of all work." Clearly, Younger's identification here signifies a conscious desire to establish a connection between herself and working-class women as opposed to the middle-class reformers with whom her birth and upbringing allied her. She would later auspiciously describe herself as "the bridge that connects working women with their wealthy sisters."[11]

Younger claimed that these same forces and experiences "made me a woman suffragist . . . I grew to know the wage-earning woman and her problems far better than I had ever known anything else, and everything I learned was one more argument for suffrage." New York's WTUL also gave her ample exposure to women members such as historian Mary Ritter Beard, journalist Rheta Childe Dorr, and suffragist Harriot Stanton Blatch, daughter of Elizabeth Cady Stanton--staunch suffragists all.[12]

In 1906, Younger returned to San Francisco. The city's residents were still reeling from the effects of the earthquake, as Younger described walking through the "silent, deserted streets" of a city which resembled a "graveyard, where nothing grew and nothing lived, and the monuments were shattered and broken." Proudly bearing a travelling union card entitling her to membership in the San Francisco local, she sought out the Waitresses' Local 48 headquarters. While officials accepted her card, Younger noticed a lack of camaraderie; that the waitresses "seemed somewhat aloof." The business agent then announced that a member was to leave for Arizona soon and asked Younger replace her at her workplace. Younger mused, "It had not been my idea to take a job in this city where I had grown up (and) . . . knew so many, but there was the situation and all the girls stopped to look at me. Confronted with being a snob, a shirk or a waitress, I chose the latter hoping it would be . . . somewhere on the outskirts of town. But when she handed me a paper with the address, it was strangely on our own property . . . in one of those temporary shack(s) such as spring up like mushrooms after the fire . . . for which we received $250 a month."[13]

In contrast with her account of the pitiful lives of the unorganized New York waitresses, Younger could hardly contain her delight and approval at working conditions in San Francisco's organized restaurants. When Younger reported for work and asked if she should wash the floors or tables, for example, the headwaitress replied, "Women don't wash floors in San Francisco." The cook's helpers, who principally washed dishes, performed all the heavy labor in the restaurants. This job qualified Younger as a full member of Local 48 and the "millionaire waitress" proceeded to involve herself with her new union and the San Francisco labor movement. According to Younger, "The union met regularly on Monday afternoons and I never missed a meeting." Her eagerness to be considered part of labor demonstrated her desire to be more than an ally. Sunset Magazine noted that Younger said that she had "left reform movements for the people to join the reform movements of the people."[14]

Younger's first documented action as a member of the labor community was a five-dollar donation to the Telephone Operators' Union during its May 1907 strike. Alice Park, the California suffrage movement's major propagandist and pamphleteer, also recalled that Younger gave her first suffrage speech at the Santa Clara Equal Suffrage convention that year. Park reminisced that, "She read from typewritten pages and her hands shook and her voice trembled."[15]

Despite that inauspicious start, Younger developed into an accomplished and impassioned public speaker. Her training came not only from orations at suffrage meetings, but from speeches before Local 48 and other labor organizations. In January of 1908, Younger, Louise LaRue, Waitresses' Union Business Agent and Vice President, and Lillian Harris Coffin, San Francisco Equal Suffrage League leader, appeared before the California Federation of Labor to present a resolution endorsing the submission of an amendment to the state constitution giving women the ballot. The resolution also asked that "all women's organizations affiliated with this organization make a specific effort to secure the passage of said amendment." Members of the United Garment Workers, Local 131, and Steam Laundry Workers Union, Local 26, also came to support the resolution. The proposal passed by a comfortable margin. Younger and Coffin spoke on woman suffrage at a Local 48 meeting later that month. The Call reported that Younger spoke before the Waitresses again in March on "topics of the day."[16]

In July 1908, the Labor Clarion reported that women from several unions came together to organize "a club for women and girls engaged in industry." Dubbed the Twentieth Century Club, the club's founders promised "educational advancement and social relaxation, ... concerts, literary societies, entertainments, reading rooms, reception and music rooms." Laundry Workers'

Labor Council Delegate L.C. Walden was named president with Louise LaRue (then Local 48's Financial Secretary, Treasurer and Labor Council Delegate,) as Vice President, and Maud Younger as Treasurer. The club had the official endorsement of the Waitresses' Union. Younger, Walden, and LaRue addressed the opening of the new club in early September.[17]

Why did Walden, LaRue and Younger feel compelled to provide a respectable club environment for wage-earning women? A number of possible reasons can explain this venture. While middle-class club women typically reached out to female wage-earners in this manner[18], perhaps unionists wanted to create a club as an extension of a working-class institution, the union. Indeed such a club could expose young workers to union activities and philosophy, continue to instill and activate a sense of community solidarity and advance the social function of the union beyond its own walls.[19] In an interview in the Call in January 1908, Younger said just this. She remarked that she and LaRue were "working very hard to establish a club for union women in the Mission. We want more unions; . . . we will model it on the line of the California Club." Younger and LaRue conferred with California Club members to "decide details of the union women's club."[20]

For Younger, her past experience in the College Settlement may have promoted an interest in such an enterprise. She derived genuine pleasure from spending her days leading the "girls" in song and conducting meetings of the resident literary club. Younger seemed to thrive in the world of female culture and society, yet she clearly preferred the company of working-class women to her peers.[21]

In late August, Younger contributed an article to the Labor Clarion entitled "Why Wage-Earning Women Should Vote." She asserted that women wage-earners often turned to unions for protection because they were "without a voice in government. . . . But the union cannot do everything. . . . If food is unpure, trust prices exorbitant, dwelling houses unsanitary, public schools bad, public hospitals poor, police protection inadequate, the rich can pay for private services. . . .The poor have no choice." Working-class women, being the most vulnerable at work and having the additional responsibility of family life, needed the vote.[22]

The following week, Younger joined LaRue and Labor Council Delegate Cora Schade as Local 48 representatives at the Republican and Democratic 1908 conventions to urge the endorsement of woman suffrage legislation. She also participated in the committee that drafted the union's new bylaws and constitution.[23]

Thus, by the time of the San Francisco Wage Earners' Suffrage League's formation on September 22, 1908, Younger and her working-class counterpart, Louise LaRue, had established themselves as labor's spokeswomen and representatives on behalf of suffrage. LaRue and Younger probably functioned as an effective team: the feminist trade-union leader and the class-conscious suffragist. They were a personification of the potential of cross-class alliances.

In addition, another union figure rose to visibility at this time. The WESL founding meeting selected Minna O'Donnell as its president. According to a brief biographical sketch in the Labor Clarion, O'Donnell trained as a printer while still "a girl" and practiced her craft in Wisconsin for seven years before marrying E.H. O'Donnell and immigrating to San Francisco with him. She was initiated into the Women's Auxiliary #18 of International Typographical Union Local 21, San Francisco's ITU affiliate and her husband's union, in September 1907. By January, 1908, O'Donnell was serving as a trustee of the organization and, in December of that year, the Women's Auxiliary nominated O'Donnell as its president. In August 1908, O'Donnell also became the Labor Clarion's official reporter on women's issues through her weekly column, "Women's Department." The Labor Clarion noted that O'Donnell was also a neighborhood activist as secretary of the Richmond Heights Improvement Club.[24]

While the names of other women would crop up periodically, this trio became the mainstay of suffrage and other socially- and politically-oriented activity among women in the labor community during this period.

At its founding meeting, the WESL (then called the Wage Earner's State League) chose vice presidents from Oakland and San Jose as well as San Francisco. It hoped to elect vice presidents from Sacramento and Los Angeles in the future and to include representatives "from every trade" in its membership. Mrs. Will French, wife of the <u>Labor Clarion</u>'s editor, became the group's treasurer. Attendees also selected a delegate to the up-coming California State Federation of Labor convention on October 5. Maud Younger did not assume an official position with the WESL at this time or at any time during the organization's life.[25]

No organizational records of the Wage Earners' Suffrage League remain. There are large gaps in the information available regarding the group and its adherents. It is not known how many unionists attended the WESL's founding meeting or what unions they represented, although O'Donnell's report claimed that "nearly all unions" sent participants. Except for LaRue, O'Donnell, and French, the officers' affiliations remain unknown.

New York's Equality League for Self-Supporting Women may have served as an inspiration for the WESL. Founded by Harriot Stanton Blatch in January 1907, the organization strove to unite professional women and women in industrial jobs into one suffrage organization. Blatch believed that these two groups of women, and not the benevolence-oriented clubwomen who dominated many Progressive organizations, should be the leaders of their sex, as self-support connoted autonomy and independence.[26] According to historian Ellen DuBois, Blatch identified work as "the basis of women's claim on the state" and regarded wage-earning women "less as victims to be succored, than as exemplars of their sex."[27]

In organizing the Equality League, Blatch created a political arm for the New York Women's Trade Union League and was given office space in the NYWTUL's suite. Unionists in the NYWTUL participated vigorously in the Equality League and lobbied the state legislature for enfranchisement on behalf of their peers. The Equality League claimed to have over nineteen thousand members by 1909, although Blatch reached this figure by counting every woman who had ever attended a meeting as well as the members of all affiliated unions. The Equality League received wide publicity in newspapers and suffrage journals, meriting praise in the Labor Clarion. Its emphasis on the necessity of including working-class women in the suffrage movement could not have missed the attention of someone like Maud Younger.[28]

The Labor Clarion did not report any further meetings of the WESL through 1908. O'Donnell's column continued to print national suffrage news and noteworthy accomplishments by women as well as union women's news of local interest and household hints. She reported Local 48's ball at Dreamland Rink to raise money for its sick benefit fund, the Twentieth Century Club's successful Halloween Ball to fund its reading rooms and headquarters, and frequent notices on the activity of the ITU Women's Auxiliary #18. She also put out a request for material for the column, which continued to appear without her byline after November.[29]

Waitresses' Local 48 elected Maud Younger as president of the union at its last meeting of 1908. In her autobiography, Younger recounted her "intense surprise" at her election. "I do not think in looking back that any honor in all my life has meant so much or been more appreciated. I should say, however, that it was not appreciated by my family. . . (The family) complained that every time they arrived or left for Europe or gave a dinner . . . the papers would announce that the Daughter (sic) or sister was President of the Waitresses' Union, and sometimes they would be interviewed on my activities."[30]

The local also chose Younger and LaRue as delegates to the San Francisco Labor Council at that same meeting. The Labor Council accepted the credentials of Younger, LaRue, and three other Local 48 delegates at its January 8, 1909 meeting. "For something like 3 years I did not miss a Friday night," Younger recalled. "There was something very vital, dynamic in the atmosphere of that smoke-filled room . . . In the corner where sat the waitresses were also teamsters, longshoremen, and some less skilled labor, great husky men, broad-shouldered, thick-necked, often scuffling, playing pranks, rough-housing good naturedly, drawing laughter from the room. With this group, I always felt most in sympathy."[31]

Lillian Coffin's 1909 report of the CESA State Central Committee included the comment that "all labor leaders" supported woman suffrage.[32] Coffin's comment reflected a growing awareness of the importance of labor support. In 1909, the National American Woman Suffrage Association recognized that it needed working-class support in order to win total suffrage for women. In that year, it reversed an earlier position which favored placing educational restrictions on suffrage, specifically to make the suffrage cause more acceptable to working-class voters and labor support. The organization also passed a resolution at its national convention endorsing the work of the AFL, which had repeatedly endorsed the notion of woman suffrage since 1903 and did so again in 1908. The NAWSA and its adherents realized that middle-class reform votes alone could not assure suffrage's victory. These changes, in conjunction with the appearance of groups such as the Equality League for Self-Supporting Women and the WESL, provided the impetus for the suffrage movement's appeals to organized labor to promote a pro-suffrage alliance.[33]

On January 8, 1909, the "Women's Department" announced that the WESL would lobby the state legislature to pass a measure which would bring woman suffrage before California voters. The column's author proclaimed, "it is high time that the thousands and thousands of women in California who desire the ballot should receive the common courtesy of having their claims presented to the citizens. This is a progressive age!"[34]

A later column noted that WESL members Louise LaRue and Maud Younger journeyed to Sacramento with John I. Nolan, the California Federation of Labor lobbyist and that the "prospects [for the amendment's passage] are good."[35]

According to Selina Solomons, pro-suffrage activists from up and down the state came to Sacramento in relay teams; one group spelling off another after a brief, intense period of pressuring legislators to vote for the proposed constitutional amendment. After five weeks of this hectic activity, suffragists suffered a crushing defeat. The Assembly vote fell fifteen votes short of that needed to carry the proposed bill. Six Assembly representatives who had supported the measure two years before reversed their votes. The resolution was not introduced in the Senate.[36]

When legislators attempted to placate the women with an offer of municipal suffrage, the infuriated feminists called for "a whole loaf of political equality or no suffrage bread at all." The decisiveness of the defeat drove home to lobbyists exactly how much work had to be done to secure a victory. "Every one of that lobby went forth as a suffrage missionary," contended Solomons. Upon the delegation's return, the Labor Clarion reported that, "The waitresses are perturbed at the failure of the legislature to pass the woman suffrage question to the referendum vote of the people of California."[37]

The WESL seems to have gone into hibernation during 1909 and 1910, as it is not mentioned at all in the labor or daily press. Its activists, however, attempted to remain in the eye of the labor community. They seemed to be casting about to find ways to interest union and other wage-earning women in becoming active on their own behalf and thus prepare them for work in the suffrage movement.

The Twentieth Century Club held a social on February 13 to raise funds for "a downtown lunch and rest room for wage-earning women." Nothing further, however, was reported on the club's existence. Later in the year, the Waitresses' Union established a reading room at its new office in the Pacific Building at Market and Fourth Streets in the heart of downtown San Francisco.[38]

Starting in 1909, however, the pages of the Labor Clarion were filled with more articles of interest to union women or the female family members of male unionists. Aside from the weekly column, now entitled "For Women in Union and Home," the Clarion reported on woman suffrage in New Zealand and Australia, the AFL's pro-suffrage position, the movement opposing child labor, and the visits of female labor dignitaries, such as Margaret Daly of the Garment Workers' Union.[39]

One article strongly endorsed woman suffrage. Written by Susan W. Fitzgerald of the Women's Union Label League, the piece declared that woman in the home was fit to vote and would insure competent and compassionate city governments, even if that meant replacing all municipal elected officials. "Women are, by nature and training, housekeepers. Let them have a hand in the city's housekeeping, even if they introduce an occasional house-cleaning," lectured Fitzgerald. The Clarion agreed, remarking in an editorial, "Men neglect certain elements of the conduct of a city just as they neglect household matters. Woman is the one to have these in charge."[40]

In a complementary article, Anne Withington called for the unionization of women, remarking that the higher wages of union women workers would raise the standard of living for all and thereby benefit society at large. The Clarion, then, took a broad view of women, depicting them in their traditional role as well as validating their position as unionists.[41]

The WESL may have been in hibernation, but business as usual proceeded for Waitresses' Local 48. The Clarion reported regularly on the doings of the Waitresses' Union. In March, 1909, Local 48 investigated a rumor that some of its members were working below the union's contracted wage scale. The report further admonished waitresses to wear their union buttons.[42]

Both LaRue and Younger served on the committee to organize a July 4th picnic. A fund-raising event to benefit the local's sick and death benefit, the picnic attracted approximately 1200 unionists to a Berkeley park. The picnic turned into an annual event for the waitresses.[43]

On July 4, as the National American Woman Suffrage Association convened its annual meeting in Seattle, a number of prominent suffragists commented on the question of the vote in the pages of the San Francisco Call. While officers of the CESA wrote on the need for a federal amendment giving women the franchise and women's civic responsibility, Maud Younger offered a piece entitled "The Wage Earners' Need of the Ballot." Younger argued that the ballot "is not so much a question of sex as of class." While union women had won many gains, the majority of women workers had no protection against working twelve-hour days or unsanitary, unsafe workplaces. Younger maintained that these women needed the ballot "more than any other women--more than any man" so that laws guaranteeing fair working conditions for women would not only be enacted, but enforced. Younger believed that union organizing provided the most effective means for changing the workplace to benefit women workers. It was, however, so difficult to unionize women that many would only see improvements on the job if they could use the ballot as a tool to demand those changes. "The wage earning woman needs the ballot because her every gain in the past has come through her own effort, and every future victory she must win for herself."[44]

Younger would continue to represent the union suffragist position in the daily and labor press, and to particularly emphasize the benefits of woman suffrage for wage-earning women at public meetings. Why she assumed this role remains a point of speculation. One explanation may be that women unionists involved in the suffrage cause did not have the time or inclination to prepare press statements and trusted Younger with this task. Certainly, Younger's public affirmation of the power of unionization on women, with the ballot as a complementary but lesser weapon for winning rights on the job, suited her for the task. Her strong characterizations of wage-earning women as potential captains of their own destinies and her belief in organized labor's primacy must have reinforced the labor movements' and union womens' trust in her. Perhaps the press sought her out as a credible and reputable spokeswoman. As a member of a prominent San Francisco family, her growing command of the pen and soapbox, and her off-beat affiliation with organized labor, her attraction as a public figure was unmistakable.

The statement printed in the Call served as a model for her future pronouncements on woman suffrage and female wage-earners. As with her July 1909 article, Younger's later statements emphasized the paid woman worker's need for the ballot in order to meet her full range of social obligations - wife, mother, wage-earner, and civic and industrial activist.

The Waitresses' Union occasionally got caught up in the personal welfare of its members. That summer, Local 48 fought for the life of one of its members, figuratively and literally. Younger and other members of the union attended the trial of one of their union sisters, Laura MacDonald, charged with murdering her two-year-old son. Despondent and destitute after being deserted by her lover, McDonald shot the child and attempted suicide on May 20. During her recovery in the hospital from the botched self-poisoning, McDonald listed the Waitresses' Union as her next-of-kin. The union, in kind, adopted McDonald and her case. Beginning in early July, Younger sat next to the twenty-one year old woman as she was tried, giving her comfort and encouragement, while other union members watched from the gallery. In early August, Local 48 held a benefit ball for McDonald's court costs and living expenses at the Dreamland Rink. When the court acquitted McDonald in September, she convalesced at Younger's home.[45]

In addition to conducting its own business and protecting its members, Local 48 participated in the activities of the local labor community. Its delegates attended Labor Council meetings and the local marched in the annual Labor Day Parade sponsored by the San Francisco Labor Council. The Waitresses stepped off in the parade's first division, Miscellaneous Trades, and won the Examiner's Cup awarded to the union women with the most presentable contingent. In addition, Executive Board members Bertha Cooper and Edith Reynolds captured a twenty-five dollar prize for the "lady unionist making the best appearance." Shortly afterward, Louise LaRue received a warm send-off as she left for Chicago and the National Women's Trade Union League Convention.[46]

The Clarion also reported Minna O'Donnell's continuing participation in the ITU Women's Auxiliary #18.[47]

In November 1909, the Union Labor Party returned to municipal power with the election of Building Trades Council President P.H. McCarthy as Mayor. The ULP also won a majority of seats on the Board of Supervisors. This must have encouraged for union suffragists like LaRue, who had supported McCarthy's candidacy since 1907. To have unionists in City Hall again offered them hope for political clout as unionists as well as women, should they win the ballot.

With regard to the fate of woman suffrage in the union movement, the most important event of 1910 was the reactivation of the San Francisco chapter of the Women's International Union Label League. Founded in 1899 as an auxiliary of the American Federation of Labor, the League existed to convince working-class women to buy only union-made goods. Through the consumption of union-label goods, the League hoped to promote its list of objectives which included shutting down the sweatshop system, winning the universal eight-hour day, abolishing child labor, equal pay for equal work, and "industrial and political equality for women." By 1910, the WIULL claimed 1,000 members nationwide, most of whom were female union members or the wives of male unionists.[48]

In San Francisco, members of the Women's Auxiliaries of the San Francisco Typographical and Varnishers and Polishers locals initiated a branch in 1905. The group met and acted sporadically until an upsurge in union label activity in 1909. That year, various articles appealed to union members in general for a "Label Revival," while some spoke exclusively to women to buy union-label goods for their families. Maud Younger even composed a song entitled "The Union Label Man," dedicated to the local Garment Worker's Union. The Labor Clarion pronounced the tune "very catchy."[49]

In October, 1909 the Clarion announced that the California WIULL had convened its first state convention in San Diego the previous week. By November, the Clarion expressed the hope that when women won the vote, they would use it to vote for the union label.[50]

The San Francisco Labor Council's minutes of March 4, 1910, announced that the Label Committee discussed forming a WIULL chapter in San Francisco. In April, the Labor Clarion featured "An Appeal to Women's Pride," asking women to join the WIULL. Three months later, union women founded the chapter, appointing Lizzie Williams of Laundry Workers Local 26 as temporary president and Sarah Hagan, president of Garment Worker's Union Local 131, as temporary secretary. Hagan also served on the San Francisco Labor Council's Label Committee.[51]

In August, members elected Lizzie Williams president, Mrs. Elinor Scharrenberg, wife of the head of the California Federation of Labor, became First Vice President. Mrs. L.C. Walden, organizer for the Steam Laundry Workers' Union and a member of the SFLC's Union Label Committee, served as Second Vice President. Hannah Mahoney Nolan, Laundry Workers organizer and wife of Bricklayer's Union official Edward L. Nolan, became Secretary-Treasurer. Trustees included Minna O'Donnell, Rose Myears of the Bindery

Women's Union No. 125, and Maud Younger, who remained a Local 48 Labor Council delegate. The group vowed to publish a folder displaying the various crafts and their respective labels with the reasons supporting the consumption of those goods bearing the label. The Clarion reported the meeting was "largely attended." The San Francisco Labor Council's Label Committee officially endorsed the chapter one week later.[52]

In its annual report in the Labor Day issue of the Clarion, Garment Workers' Union Local 131 called upon the labor community to demand the union label to aid its membership. Later that month, Hannah Nolan reported that she had visited forty-four labor organizations to promote the purpose of the WIULL and, in addition, called on unions to support the notion of a female factory inspector in San Francisco. Nolan's presentations were well received, according to the Labor Clarion. Elinor Scharrenberg represented the chapter, now known as WIULL Local #258, at the California Federation of Labor's convention in early October.[53]

For the remainder of the year, Local 258 continued to pursue its goals and maintain its visibility by sending speakers to events such as the California Equal Suffrage Association convention and Labor Council meetings, conducting meetings, and printing notices in the Labor Clarion. Even Organized Labor, the organ of the Building Trades Council, printed an article on the organization written by Mrs. Frances A. Williamson, the Oakland WIULL president. The Labor Clarion also listed the group as an official labor organization.[54]

Sherry Katz has noted that the California WIULL's program surpassed that of the national organization in terms of political and social breadth and involvement, and had a more feminist orientation. While the national organization rarely moved beyond its union label campaign and what Katz characterized as its "bland call for 'social and political equality,'" the state structure took on the suffrage issue, praised the NWTUL's efforts to organize women in New York's garment industry and promoted the passage of eight-hour work day legislation for California women. WIULL Local 258's platform reportedly mirrored these differences. For these positions and actions, the California League earned the enmity of national President Annie Fitzgerald and was denied full recognition by the International League.[55]

Younger and O'Donnell kept a low profile in the WIULL, while LaRue apparently did not participate at all. The garment and laundry unions seemed to predominate in the organization's top leadership, as they did in the Los Angeles chapter, and Hannah Nolan stepped forward to represent the group publicly in most instances. Younger, meanwhile, continued to speak out in favor of votes for wage-earning women, appearing in an afternoon program on suffrage with CESA President Elizabeth Lowe Watson and Berkeley's socialist Mayor J. Stitt Wilson in February at the Golden Gate Commandery Building.[56]

Suffragist Mary McHenry Keith reported that Watson herself also began appearing before labor unions in this year, in addition to making the rounds of clubs and churches. This indicated an increased interest by the CESA in union endorsements and support. On top of this, reform suffrage leaders appeared to pay more attention to working-class women. The College Equal Suffrage League opened its membership to "all women" in 1910. Selina Solomons organized the Votes for Women Club in a downtown office, hoping to attract women working in the district's offices and shops, as well as at the major department stores. Club headquarters boasted an economical lunchroom and comfortable reading area, well stocked with suffrage literature.[57]

The November 1910 elections brought the national suffrage movement a needed shot in the arm -- the first state victory for women's enfranchisement in fourteen years. On November 8, Washington state voters approved a referendum granting suffrage to its female citizens by a two-to-one margin. The Washington triumph broke the logjam and lifted the hopes of suffragists from coast to coast. While the success in Washington was cause for celebration, however, the movement required a victory in a major, influential state to truly get the momentum rolling. Since the West provided the most fertile ground for such an achievement, eyes turned to California to provide the seed for a revitalized campaign.[58]

In mid-January, 1911, California suffragists made their biennial trip to Sacramento. This year, however, the outcome would be different. The reformist Lincoln-Roosevelt League dominated the Republican Party, wresting control from the Southern Pacific machine in the newly-initiated primaries in the summer of 1910. Progressives occupied the party's platform committee, the legislature, and the governor's seat. While Governor Hiram Johnson held a lukewarm position on woman suffrage, platform committee members Chester Rowell, publisher of the Fresno Morning Republican, and John H. Braly, an entrepreneur from Los Angeles, strongly supported the issue. When the party's 1910 platform appeared, it included a plank recommending the submission of a constitutional amendment enfranchising women to a public referendum. The Republicans had finally endorsed woman suffrage.[59]

Younger and LaRue again joined the suffrage contingent that trooped to the state capital for hearings on the amendment. Younger alone testified for the Wage Earner's Suffrage League, delivering what must have been a familiar speech on the value of suffrage to California's female wage-earners. Despite vigorous testimony from a delegation of anti-suffragists, the resolution passed without a hitch in both the Senate and Assembly. On February 2, 1911, the California state legislature turned over the momentous decision of whether or not women should cast a ballot to the state's male voters. Presented as one in a package of twenty-three amendments to the state constitution, woman suffrage came before the California electorate in a special election called for October 10, 1911.[60]

As with other suffrage clubs, 1911 was a frantic year of activity for the League. Soon after the Legislature voted on Amendment Eight, Younger and LaRue returned to Sacramento with Hannah Nolan to lobby for the eight-hour day for California's women workers. The Oregon ten-hour day law for women provided a model for this legislation. Declared constitutional by the United States Supreme Court in 1908 in Muller v. Oregon, the measure stood at the vanguard of the era's protective legislation. Nolan testified about her long hours of exposure to lint in the laundries and the high incidence of tuberculosis among laundry workers while LaRue related that "the average waitress walks ten miles a day" which was almost as much as an army mule was allowed to walk in the same time. Both labor and Progressive organizations supported this measure, which passed both houses of the state legislature easily in March, 1911.[61]

The campaign for the act did not proceed without incident, however. On March 2, Lillian Harris Coffin declared herself opposed to the proposed eight-hour day bill by actively supporting a compromise measure which substituted a ten-hour day as a more reasonable demand on behalf of women workers. Coffin maintained that the ten-hour day stood a better chance of weathering a legal challenge in the courts because of its similarity to Muller v. Oregon. To further reinforce her position, Coffin produced a letter from the NWTUL president Margaret Dreier Robins endorsing the ten-hour day bill and criticizing those who promoted the unrealistic eight-hour version as "ignorant of their aid and comfort to the enemies of the working people." Certainly, Coffin comforted herself with the thought that she represented the more rational and practical view, but to the labor-oriented Daily News, and most probably its readership, Coffin's perspective and her actions revealed once again her lack of concern for solidarity with labor and, in particular, with her working-class sisters.[62]

The WESL held public meetings such as one on May 16 at the Central Theater which featured speakers such as San Francisco Mayor P.H. McCarthy, Labor Clarion editor Will French, and John I. Nolan, legislative agent for the California State Federation of Labor. Louise LaRue, elected president of Local 48 soon afterward, introduced the speakers and Minna O'Donnell chaired the meeting. The Labor Clarion reported "good attendance" and noted that granting women suffrage was "an act of simple justice."[63]

In July 1911, the Labor Council granted the WESL "credentials to visit unions on the subject of suffrage," giving the it increased legitimacy and credence.[64] The Labor Clarion then listed the League in its official roster of unions and organizations, along with the Women's Union Label League. The listing included the League's hours, 9 to 11 a.m. daily, and identified Louise LaRue as secretary. The WESL office was located in the Labor Temple along with the Labor Council's headquarters.[65]

In order to coordinate the statewide publicity effort in the campaign's final months, the California Equal Suffrage Association selected representatives from five suffrage organizations to serve on a State Central Committee in early August 1911. Younger represented the Wage Earners' Suffrage League on this committee, which included leaders of the Woman's Suffrage Party, Club Women's Franchise League, and College Equal Suffrage League.[66]

Each constituent group on the Central Committee produced its own campaign literature which was then distributed by the CESA. A spare, direct leaflet written by Maud Younger entitled "Why Working Women Should Vote" addressed the suffrage issue from the WESL's perspective. Focusing on the recent Eight Hour Day Law for Women, the piece urged voters to support Amendment Eight so that women could use their political clout to insure the law's implementation and enforcement. This flyer portrayed women primarily as workers and civic activists on their own behalf, while alluding to their responsibilities in the home.[67]

On August 13, Younger and LaRue returned from a two-week lecture tour of San Jose and Stockton. The pair visited three Central Labor Councils and proudly announced that they had reached men who would not go to suffrage meetings. LaRue spoke plainly to the unionists, saying "We are your own women who are asking you to do this for us. Every member of our league is a union woman." She pointed out that the ballot most greatly benefited working women "who after all comprise the largest class of women in California" and showed how the possession of the ballot would not interfere with the home.[68]

By the end of August, the League had visited seventy-eight unions and obtained endorsements from "nearly everyone." The majority of these unions endorsed suffrage unanimously. WESL speakers included Younger, O'Donnell, LaRue, and Edith Reynolds of Local 48, Mrs. L.C. Walden and Lizzie Williams of the Steam Laundry Workers, and Daisy Mank of the Cracker Bakers' Auxiliary Union. These women routinely attended three to six union meetings in an evening. To Younger, the most important endorsement came from the Brewery Workers' Union despite strong opposition to the Amendment from liquor interests based on the long-standing connection between the suffrage and temperance movements. The League laid plans to visit forty more unions and to conduct meetings in the streets, in shops and in factories. While some of these events were geared to engage working-class men, such as a planned visit to the Union Iron Works, the meetings also targeted working women on their lunch hour. Younger also reported that the WESL had established branches in Los Angeles, Richmond, and San Jose.[69]

The Call's article on the WESL's progress also noted that "Many working women who are unable to do more than attend to their employment during the day are volunteering to work at night, speaking before organizations or doing whatever they can to serve the vote." For wage-earning women, then, involvement in the WESL meant sacrificing their evenings after spending their days at work. Unlike many middle-class suffragists, who enjoyed their husbands' financial support or had independent means, union suffragists put in a "double shift" to work for woman suffrage. These activists included members of the Waitresses' Union, other than Younger and LaRue, the Steam Laundry Workers' Union and the Cracker Bakers' Auxiliary, including former waitress Laura MacDonald.[70]

Younger and LaRue described a typical opportunity to appeal for woman suffrage at a union meeting in the August 17 edition of the <u>San Francisco Daily News</u>. Although their organization bore the Labor Council's stamp of approval, they were frequently sequestered in a union hall's anteroom until the local passed judgement on their credentials. The "pretty" LaRue, as the reporter described her, explained, "It is all we can do to get up the courage to go in and talk after all we have heard through the closed doors. You see, these are men who have not gone to the suffrage meetings held by the various clubwomen, and who don't want to go. If they won't listen to us they won't have the amendment presented to them at all."[71]

On this particular evening, however, the duo had no trouble gaining entrance to the monthly meeting of the Carpenters Union, Local 438. Shortly after Younger passed the WESL's credentials through a slot in the door, the membership elected to hear them. As they stepped into the hall, the entire assembly rose to its feet and remained standing until Younger and LaRue took their seats.[72]

Both women spoke that night. Younger reminded the men of the significance of the eight-hour day law for women and female wage-earners desire for political clout. "We women realize that the ballot is a protection because we see what it has done for the men. Look at the way we women who work went up to Sacramento and fought for the eight-hour day by staying on the ground, and appealing to the men day and night without pause." The vote, Younger admonished, would begin to rectify the inequality women faced in the courts, as when women were given stiffer penalties for picketing than men, by increasing the amount of social power they wielded.[73]

LaRue stressed that it was their union sisters and other wage-earning women, not clubwomen or society ladies, who would benefit most from woman suffrage. "I come before you as a wage-earner. The members of the Wage Earners' Suffrage League are all union women, and do you realize that there are

4000 union women in San Francisco asking for the ballot because they know it will help them toward their rights as it has helped you men? Most of you are prejudiced against suffrage because it seems to be the interest of club and society women whom you do not know. You say,'These are not our women' when you see their picture in the paper. But we also are asking for the ballot, and asking it not as a whim or fad of the moment."[74]

The evening ended as others had for Younger and LaRue, with a pledge of endorsement from the leadership of the union. The union president assured them while shaking their hands, "When the month rolls round, I can promise you that every man in local 483 is going to go out and vote for that amendment for you girls." Said LaRue of the encounters with their union brothers in general, "We have never at any union in San Francisco been interrupted or treated discourteously. Most of them have been interested. Some have endorsed us without waiting for any later formality, and nearly all of them have promised to endorse us."[75]

Interestingly, both LaRue and Younger represented themselves as working women. At one point in the presentation, Younger drove the point home by referring to herself as a union woman, which was technically true. It seemed important to Younger to represent herself as a wage-earner and unionist, even though she had apparently not taken up her apron and tray for almost five years. Seemingly, she felt that her brief experience as a waitress had permanently left its stamp on her personal and class identity, and validated her presence in the labor community. The news report reinforced this by referring to her as only as a Local 48 member. As she had wished before, Younger now spoke not for working women, but with them and as one of them.[76]

In the last week of August, suffragists participated in Women's Day festivities at the California State Fair in Sacramento. In Oak Park on August 25, LaRue and Younger joined other prominent suffrage leaders on the platform at a rally which three thousand enthusiastic supporters attended.[77]

The WESL rounded out the week with a night meeting at the Valencia Theater in the Mission district on August 31. The Examiner described the hall as "crowded to the doors" as Mayor J. Stitt Wilson of Berkeley joined San Francisco's P.H. McCarthy to pledge their support for Amendment Eight. LaRue introduced McCarthy as "the only candidate for mayor [in San Francisco] who has had the nerve to say he is for woman suffrage." McCarthy faced a stiff challenge at the polls in September from James Rolph, Jr., a fusion candidate of the Democratic and Republican parties, who took no position on woman suffrage.[78]

The Labor Day issue of the Labor Clarion featured an article by Maud Younger entitled, "Why the Ballot is Needed by Women." Younger depicted women as wage-earners who had followed the work of the household into the factory with the advent of industrialization. She reiterated that when these women crossed the threshold of the workplace, they existed not "as wife, mother or home-maker but as wage-earner." As such, they needed the dual protection of union and ballot, "the same sources of strength as have men." To deny them the political clout of the ballot would serve as a continuing threat to women's own health, to organized labor and to the community at large. Aside from the obvious assault of a noxious workplace and a long workday on women's bodies, union gains could be undermined by a cheap female labor force. The future of society as a whole hung in the balance, according to Younger, when physically weakened women became the "mothers of the race." In this final piece of propaganda, Younger characterized women as intrinsically linked with wage-earning. Their ability to regulate the conditions of their own labor, through the union and the vote had vast societal consequences. The male electorate denied female workers full citizenship at their own peril.[79]

The WESL's campaign reached its tactical zenith on September 4, when the League and the Waitresses' Union sponsored an impressive float in the San Francisco Labor Day Parade. Starting in the Mission District, the throng of thousands of marching unionists surged to Van Ness Street and down Market Street to the Embarcadero, which ran along the waterfront rim. The WESL float, drawn by six black horses and festooned with yellow streamers, brought up the rear of the first division of marchers. Younger sat in the driver's seat, holding the horses' reins. Behind her, women dressed in the uniforms of their trade or occupation performed their on-the-job duties as cannery workers, nurses, sewing machine operators, academics, shop girls and clericals, while a woman in Grecian robes (a representation of the California state seal) handed a ballot to one of these women. Shields mounted on the sides of the float proclaimed, "These Women Need The Vote," " Votes For Mother, Too," and "Justice For Women."[80]

According to the San Francisco Call, the crowd lining the streets "heartily cheered" the float as it rolled towards the waterfront. As it passed the reviewing stand at Market and California Streets, Parade Grand Marshall Samuel Gompers, president of the American Federation of Labor, saluted the float. Later, Gompers delivered a strong endorsement of Amendment Eight during his Labor Day oration.[81]

The float came to a halt at the foot of Market Street and the women held an impromptu rally. "The sincerity of the appeal, the plain, tired faces of some of the women reached men who know what it is to work for wages, and know what it is to ask for a withheld right," noted the College Equal Suffrage League's accounting of the open-air meeting. The float's inhabitants then joined the rest of the day's celebrants as they crossed San Francisco Bay on a ferry to Shellmound Park in the East Bay to hear Gompers' speech.[82]

Two San Francisco newspapers featured pictures of the lavish float which received an "Honorable Mention" from the reviewing stand judges. The float clearly produced its intended effect, publicizing the convictions of the union suffragists, and reaching out directly to male wage-earning voters. The College Equal Suffrage League, which had contributed the design and absorbed some of the float's expenses, later exclaimed, "Our yellow challenge ran through the people's coolness like a hot iron through water, and raised a passing mist of passion from the crowd." [83]

Suffragists wrapped up the campaign aimed at unionists and workers in general with a meeting at the Valencia Theater sponsored by the Woman's Committee of the San Francisco Socialist Party on October 6. The Labor Clarion promoted the meeting and all interested in the cause of woman suffrage were urged to bring "their wavering friends." Maud Younger and John I. Nolan addressed the crowd inside, which packed the theater, but a huge mob still massed outside the doors. In order not to disappoint them, the speakers held a second overflow meeting outdoors "to satisfy the throng outside the theater."[84]

However, despite the valiant efforts of the Wage Earner's Suffrage League and the other San Francisco suffrage organizations, San Francisco men voted down Amendment Eight by a margin of 13,559 ballots cast (see Table 14). Had it not been for Los Angeles and the rural vote, the Amendment would have gone down to defeat. Suffrage carried by almost 4,000 votes in Protestant, southern California, where progressivism and temperance had made stronger inroads.[85]

The measure barely passed by 3,000 votes statewide, equivalent to one vote per district. Although some contended that suffrage had ridden in on the coattails of the other victorious measures on the October ballot, Mary McHenry Keith of the Political Equality League credited it as "a victory of the women and by the women," charging the progressives did not "support equal suffrage with the same strong effort that (was) applied to the other amendments." Other amendments on the ballot in the special election, such as the initiative and referendum measures passed easily in contrast to woman suffrage.[86]

A closer look at the 1911 San Francisco vote on Amendment Eight demonstrates that simplistic analyses of the defeat which point the finger of blame toward the city's working-class, immigrant, Catholic character are unconvincing.[87]   The male electorate defeated Amendment Eight in every assembly district. In looking at the vote by neighborhood, however, those areas with predominantly working-class residents cast a higher percentage of affirmative votes than any other neighborhood. (See Table 14 and 15) The South-of-Market region, home to the bulk of the city's wage-earning population, extended from the factory district below Market Street through the largely Irish Mission and Outer Mission Districts and parts of the Sunset District. The assembly districts in this area housed all types of skilled, semi-skilled and unskilled workers. Forty-two percent of those casting their votes on Amendment Eight South-of-Market voted in favor of women's enfranchisement.[88]

The city's artisanal suburbs west of the Mission, where the highly skilled workers in the building trades and workmen turned entrepreneurs resided, constituted Assembly Districts Thirty-four through Thirty-six. Mayor P.H. McCarthy called this area his home. Forty percent of those voting on Amendment Eight in these districts checked "Yes" on their ballot.[89]

In comparison, slightly more than thirty-seven percent of voters in the professional and middle-class assembly districts of the Western Addition and Richmond areas of San Francisco voted pro-suffrage. Supposedly the bastion of Progressive support, only little more than one in three men voting in these districts expressed their approval of woman suffrage at the ballot box. Similarly, the downtown area housed a large percentage of white-collar employees who worked in retail and financial establishments. The men of Assembly Districts Forty-Two and Forty-Three cast 36.4 percent of their ballots for Amendment Eight.[90]

TABLE 14

SAN FRANCISCO ELECTION RESULTS: AMENDMENT EIGHT

Neighborhood	Assembly Districts	For Amendment	Against Amendment
South-of-Market	28 - 33	5825 (42.0%)	8196 (58.0%)
Artisan Suburbs	34 - 36	4836 (40.0%)	7144 (59.6%)
Fillmore-Richmond	37 - 40	8052 (37.4%)	13,417 (62.6%)
Pacific Heights	41	1141 (32.5%)	2371 (67.5%)
Downtown	42 - 43	1234 (36.4%)	2158 (63.6%)
Waterfront	44 - 45	758 (24.4%)	2349 (75.6%)
TOTAL VOTE		21,919 (38.1%)	35,635 (61.9%)

Source: San Francisco, Board of Supervisors, San Francisco Municipal Reports for the Fiscal Year 1911-12 Ending June 30, 1912 (San Francisco: Neal Publishing Co., 1913), 231.

Assembly District breakdown into neighborhoods is based on information from the following sources:

Jules Tygiel, "'Where Unionism Holds Undisputed Sway'-- A Reappraisal of San Francisco's Union Labor Party," California History 62 (Fall 1983): 207; Robert W. Cherny and William Issel, San Francisco 1865-1932 (Berkeley and Los Angeles: University of California Press, 1986), 58-79.

TABLE 15

VOTES FOR AMENDMENT EIGHT COMPARED TO TOTAL VOTE, 1911

Classification	Assembly Districts	Vote Supporting Amendment Eight	Total Vote on Amendment Eight	Difference of Percentage
Working Class	28-36	10,761 (49.1%)	26,101 (45.4%)	3.7%
Middle Class/ White Collar	37-40,42,43	9,259 (42.2%)	24,834 (43.2%)	-1.0%
Wealthy	41	1,141 (5.2%)	3,512 (6.1%)	- .9%
Waterfront	44,45	758 (3.5%)	3,107 (5.4%)	-1.9%
		21,919 (100%)	57,554 (100%)	

Sources: San Francisco, Board of Supervisors, Municipal Reports 1911-1912, 231; Tygiel, "'Where Unionism Holds Undisputed Sway,'", 207; Issel and Cherny, San Francisco, 1865-1932, 58-79.

The wealthy and waterfront districts brought up the rear. Slightly more than thirty-two percent of the men residing in the sumptuous Pacific Heights neighborhood voted for woman suffrage. The residents of the waterfront districts which included Chinatown, North Beach, the sailors, transients of the Embarcadero and the denizens of the bawdy Barbary Coast defeated Amendment Eight by a three-to-one margin.[91]

The bulk of affirmative votes for Amendment Eight were cast in the districts identified as working class. Almost half of the votes in favor of woman suffrage came from the South-of-Market districts and the artisanal suburbs (See Table 14). Middle-class men of the Fillmore-Richmond and downtown areas followed closely behind with 42.2 percent of their ballots in favor of Amendment Eight; however, the total number of affirmative votes from these districts numbered over fifteen hundred less than those from working-class districts. It is also true, however, that almost half of the votes opposing woman suffrage came from these districts of workers. As Table 15 shows, the working-class districts, which cast 45.4% of the total votes of the election, accounted for 49.1% of the affirmative vote on Amendment Eight. Middle and upper-class districts comprising 49.3% of the electorate cast only 47.4% of their votes for suffrage. It appears, then, that the defeat of Amendment Eight in San Francisco rested as much, if not more with middle-class districts as with their working-class counterparts.

When compared with the vote count of the 1896 ballot measure for women suffrage, however, the 1911 results take on a new significance. Votes affirming woman suffrage exhibited the greatest increase in working-class districts. Approximately one quarter of those casting ballots in the South-of-Market and artisanal districts voted for woman suffrage in 1896. By 1911, pro-suffrage voters in the same areas rose to forty percent or more of the turnout in those districts. Indeed, the South-of-Market neighborhood demonstrated the highest proportion of votes for Amendment Eight in San Francisco. While the affirmative vote increased in other districts, the gains were not as dramatic as those of the pro-labor neighborhoods. (See Table 16)

In an election as close as that of 1911, many factors could account for a shift resulting in a loss or victory. Arguably, the increase of support for woman suffrage in working-class districts tipped the scales in favor of victory for Amendment Eight on the statewide level. While the WESL cannot take full credit for this shift, it was certainly a significant factor in its attempts to focus and mobilize unions' prosuffrage sentiments. More research is needed to answer further questions concerning support for woman suffrage from the different sectors of the population and what generated this support.

Still, Amendment Eight failed to carry working-class districts. Some of the factors leading to its defeat are clear. For one thing, not all of labor's adherents were prosuffrage. Father Peter Yorke, the fiercely prounion Catholic priest and important influence on the city's Irish-Catholic working class, was at best ambivalent about suffrage. "If the good ladies who are going all over the State speaking on the rights of women . . . would dwell for a little on the other glories of womanhood, I cannot help thinking they would do far more good," Yorke mused.[92] The newspaper he published, The Leader, was more direct, condemning women who spoke for suffrage as "masculine" and "illogical." Another article charged that women did not want the vote and would use it poorly, if at all.[93] Yorke's statements probably had some impact on San Francisco's high percentage of Catholic residents.[94]

Again, the liquor issue played a role. Many German and Irish immigrants feared that women might vote for prohibition and deprive them of their social customs as well as their livelihoods, according to feminist Eva Bary.[95] German language newspapers in California, sympathetic to kinsmen who brewed beer or owned saloons, opposed woman suffrage.[96] One of the allies of the Union Labor Party was the Knights of the Royal Arch, an association of twelve thousand liquor dealers. Mary McHenry Keith claimed in an article in the San Francisco

TABLE 16

SAN FRANCISCO ELECTION RESULTS:
1896 AND 1911 WOMAN SUFFRAGE AMENDMENTS

Neighborhood	Assembly Districts	1896 Vote For Amendment	1911 Vote For Amendment
South-of-Market	28 - 33	3312 (23.9%)	5925 (42.0%)
Artisan Suburbs	34 - 36	2869 (25.3%)	4836 (40.0%)
Fillmore-Richmond	37 - 40	3692 (26.2%)	6025 (37.4%)
Pacific Heights/Marina	41	886 (26.1%)	1141 (32.3%)
Downtown	42 - 43	1414 (28.9%)	1234 (36.4%)
Waterfront	44 - 45	3896 (21.1%)	758 (24.4%)
TOTAL VOTE		12,969 (26.1%)	21,919 (38.1%)

Sources: State of California, Secretary of State, Elections and Political Reform Division, General Election Returns, 3 November 1896, California State Archives, Sacramento, CA; San Francisco, Board of Supervisors, Municipal Reports, 1911-1912, 231; Tygiel,"'Where Unionism Holds Undisputed Sway,'" 207; Issel and Cherny, San Francisco, 1865-1932, 58-79.

Examiner that the Knights had a fund of $250,000 to fight woman suffrage because of its association with temperance.[97] In her unpublished history of the fifteen-year California suffrage effort, Keith again cites the liquor interests' persistent opposition and the alliance between suffrage organizations and the Women's Christian Temperance League's Franchise Department to counteract it.[98] The liquor interests surely exploited this relationship.

In its October 20 issue, the Clarion congratulated women on winning the vote. "The women of California have always been good housekeepers, and they demonstrated after the disaster of 1906 that they were also good campkeepers," the Labor Clarion editorialized. "Now that they are entitled to the ballot, they will undoubtedly prove that they are capable statekeepers."[99]

NOTES TO CHAPTER THREE

1.   Selina Solomons, How We Won the Vote in California: A True Story of the Campaign of 1911 (San Francisco: The New Woman Publishing Co., n.d.), 7.

2.   Mary McHenry Keith, "California in 1901-1920". Keith-McHenry-Pond Papers, Carton 3, File "Woman Suffrage Campaign in California", Bancroft Library, Berkeley, California; Ida Husted Harper, The History of Woman Suffrage, Volume 6, 1900 - 1920 (New York: National American Woman Suffrage Association, 1922), 32.

3.   Harper, The History of Woman Suffrage, 6: 53.

4.   Eleanor Flexner, "Maud Younger" in Edward T. James, Janet Wilson James and Paul S. Boyer, ed. Notable American Women 1607-1950, vol. 3 (Cambridge: Belknap Press, 1971), 699-700; Maud Younger, "Along The Way - Childhood in San Francisco, Growing Up, San Francisco in the 'Nineties," unpublished autobiography, National Women's Party Papers: Part II, Containers 195-196, Library of Congress, Washington, D.C. Younger's autobiography presents a problem with regard to documentation because it is not paginated. The chapter headings are only consistent identification one can use. Therefore, in this and all future citations, passages taken from the autobiography are identified by these chapter headings, which follow the work's title, as above.

5.   James, James and Boyer, Notable American Women, 3: 699; Allen F. Davis, Spearheads for Reform: The Social Settlements and The Progressive Movement, 1890-1914; (New Brunswick: Rutgers University Press, 1984), 11-12; Vera Edmondson, "Feminist and Laborite," Sunset Magazine (June 1915): 1179.

6.   Edmondson, "Feminist and Laborite," 1179-80; Inez Haynes Irwin, "Adventures of Yesteryear," unpublished autobiography, Inez H. Irwin papers, Schlesinger Library, Radcliffe College, Cambridge, Mass., 307; Maud Younger, "Along The Way - In a NY Settlement;" Edmondson, "Feminist and Laborite", 1180.

7.   Maud Younger, "The Diary of an Amateur Waitress: An Industrial Problem from the Worker's Point of View," McClure's Magazine (March, April 1907): 542-552, 665-677.

8.   Younger, "Diary of an Amateur Waitress," 549-550. Kathy Peiss has documented the negotiations between men and women in the "public, heterosexual world of commercial amusements" in which women exchanged "sexual forms of varying degrees for male attention, gifts and a good time." Peiss quotes sociologist Frances Donovan who reported that waitresses she interviewed at the turn of the century "talk(ed) about their engagements which they had for the evening or night and quite frankly saying what they expected to get from this or that fellow in the line of money, amusements or clothes." Younger's reaction to information such as this was acute embarrassment, but to many waitresses and other working women, reaping the benefits of being a "charity girl," as they were called, was a fact of life.   Kathy Peiss, Cheap Amusements: Working Women and Leisure in Turn-of-the-Century New York (Philadelphia: Temple University Press, 1986), 88-114.

9.   Younger, "Diary of an Amateur Waitress," 552.

10.   Younger, "The Diary of an Amateur Waitress," 675-677.

11.   Nancy Schrom Dye, As Equals and As Sisters (Columbia: University of Missouri Press, 1980), 42-3, 55, 63; Younger, "Along The Way - Living in a Tenement;" San Francisco Call, 8 January 1908.   In her portrayal of Margaret Dreier Robins, a founder of the NWTUL, Elizabeth Anne Payne remarked that both Robins and the NWTUL "exemplified an urge among socially conscious, well-to-do Americans to bridge the gap between themselves and wage earners." Certainly Younger was typical of this impulse.   Elizabeth Anne Payne, Reform, Labor, and Feminism: Margaret Dreier Robins and the Women's Trade Union League (Urbana and Chicago: University of Illinois Press, 1988), 2.

12.   Schrom Dye, As Equals and As Sisters, 39; New York Times, 28 June 1936.

13.   Maud Younger, "Taking Orders: A Day as a Waitress in a San Francisco Restaurant," Sunset Magazine (October 1908): 518; Maud Younger, "Along the Way -President of the Waitresses' Union."   Several accounts of Younger's life report her arrival time in San Francisco incorrectly. The autobiography pinpoints this detail accurately.

14.   Younger, "Taking Orders," 519; Irwin, "Adventures of Yesteryear," 308; Younger, "Along The Way - President of the Waitresses' Union;" Younger, "Taking Orders," 518.

15.   Labor Clarion, 31 May 1907; Alice L. Park, "Maud Younger of S.F., Washington, D.C. & Los Gatos," One-page typescript, 19 May 1943, Suffrage-U.S. Biography Subject Collection, Sophia Smith Collection, Smith College,

Northampton, Mass. For an account of the Telephone Operators' Union and the 1907 strike, see Rebecca J. Mead, "Trade Unionism and Political Activity Among Wage-Earning Women in San Francisco, 1900-1922" (M.A. thesis: San Francisco State University, 1991), 86-88.

16.   San Francisco Examiner, 10 January 1908; San Francisco Chronicle, 11 January 1908; Labor Clarion, 24 January 1908; Call, 12 March 1908.

17.   Labor Clarion, 31 July; 18 September 1908.

18.   For examples of this activity among middle-class club women, see Karen Blair, The Clubwoman as Feminist: True Womanhood Redefined, 1868-1914 (New York: Holmes & Meier Publishers, Inc., 1980), 73-92; Kathy Peiss, Cheap Amusements: Working Women and Leisure in Turn-of-the-Century New York (Philadelphia: Temple University Press, 1986), 163-184; Joanne J. Meyerowitz, Women Adrift: Independent Wage-Earners in Chicago, 1880-1930 (Chicago: University of Chicago Press, 1988), 43-55.

19.   Call, 8 January 1908. Rebecca Mead identified the Twentieth Century Club as an attempt by working-class women to form "extended support groups which provided important social opportunities and fellowship. . ." Rebecca Mead, "Trade Unionism and Political Activity Among Wage-Earning Women, 1900-1922," 15.

20.   Call, 8 January 1908. In this same interview, Younger identified herself as a socialist. The article reported that her "socialistic ideas" prevented her from joining the California Club, which she considered too temperate, and from "speaking with any moderation upon the question of capital and labor." Younger rarely publicized her sympathy with socialism, but persistently stressed her belief in trade unionism as the foremost strategy to promote the rights of wage-earning women. She later explained her position in a 1911 interview in Revolt, a San Francisco socialist weekly paper published between 1911-1912. Younger remarked that working women concerned themselves mainly with day-to-day issues, and not with long-term programs. The ULP's ascendancy and P.H. McCarthy's election as mayor in 1909 also reduced interest in socialism and other alternative forms of social change. Younger saw her approach as a pragmatic response to these notions and conditions, but one that genuinely furthered the advance of the working class. In assessing Younger's intentions, reporter Caroline Nelson complained that Younger foolishly attempted to be "all things to all women everywhere." Nelson derided Younger's advocacy of McCarthy and concluded by accusing her of pandering to the short-sighted impulses of her followers, rather than leading them with socialism's more radical and advanced message. Revolt, 30 September 1911. For a more general discussion of labor's attitude toward socialism and radicalism, see Michael Kazin,

Barons of Labor: The San Francisco Building Trades and Union Power in the
Progressive Era (Urbana and Chicago: University of Illinois Press, 1986),149-
150.

21.   For the classic article on female culture and community at the turn of the
century, see Carroll Smith-Rosenberg, "The Female World of Love and Ritual:
Relations Between Women in Nineteenth Century America," Signs 1 (Autumn
1975): 1-29.

22.   Labor Clarion, 21 August 1908.

23.   Labor Clarion, 28 August 1908; Rodes, "The California Suffrage
Campaign of 1911," 38-39.

24.   Labor Clarion, 28 August 1908; 6 September 1907; 10 January 1908; 11
December 1908; 7 August 1908.   The ITU Women's Auxiliaries' membership
consisted primarily of women "whose entire time is occupied in the care of the
home."   The Auxiliaries entertained female union members and the wives of
male members at the ITU conventions.   They also helped conduct a campaign to
promote the union label.   As of 1911, the Auxiliaries claimed 1200 members
nationally.   International Typographical Union, Fifty-Seventh Convention: San
Francisco (San Francisco: Williams Printing Co., 1911), n.p.   The San Francisco
Labor Archives and Research Center at San Francisco State University houses
a broken collection of commemorative books of ITU conventions between 1903
and 1983.

25.   Labor Clarion, 25 September 1908.

26.   Ellen Carol DuBois, "Working Women, Class Relations, and Suffrage
Militance: Harriot Stanton Blatch and the New York Suffrage Movement, 1894-
1909," Journal of American History 74 (June 1987): 47-49.

27.   DuBois, "Working Women, Class Relations, and Suffrage Militance," 48,
42.

28.   DuBois, "Working Women, Class Relations, and Suffrage Militance," 48-
49; Labor Clarion, 9 April, 1909; 14 January 1910.   According to Blatch, the
organization changed its name to the Women's Political Union in 1910 in an
effort to attract more members, although it continued to exclude women who
were not self-supporting.   In 1916, the group affiliated with the Congressional
Union, a militant national suffrage organization, in order to work for a federal
amendment for woman suffrage.   By then, Maud Younger had also joined the
Union.   Harriot Stanton Blatch and Alma Lutz, Challenging Years: The Memoirs

of Harriot Stanton Blatch (New York: G.P. Putnam & Sons, 1940), 136, 239-240.

29.   Labor Clarion, 2 October - 20 November 1908, 27 November 1908. The possibility exists that Maud Younger acted as a "ghost writer" for the column after O'Donnell's withdrawal.

30.   Labor Clarion, 1 January 1909; Younger, "Along The Way - President of the Waitresses' Union."

31.   Labor Clarion, 15 January 1909; Maud Younger, "Along The Way - Militant Labor, Dynamite and Golden Rule."

32.   Keith, "California 1901-1920".

33.   Bruce Dancis, "Socialism and Women in the United States, 1900-1917," Socialist Revolution   6 (January-March 1976): 117; Labor Clarion, 16 July, 1909.

34.   Labor Clarion, 8 January 1909.

35.   Labor Clarion, 22 January 1909.

36.   Solomons, How We Won the Vote in California, 10-11; Donald Waller Rodes, "The California Woman Suffrage Campaign of 1911" (M.A. thesis, California State University, Hayward, 1974), 39-40.

37.   Solomons, How We Won the Vote in California, 11; Labor Clarion, 12 February 1909.

38.   Labor Clarion, 26 January, 19 February, 13 August 1909.

39.   Labor Clarion, 1909-1911 passim.

40.   Labor Clarion, 24 September 1909, 15 October 1909.

41.   Labor Clarion, 2 July 1909.

42.   Labor Clarion, 26 March 1909.

43.   Labor Clarion, 25 June 1909; Call, 5 July 1909. The local also assessed each member fifteen cents per month for the death benefit. Labor Clarion, 12 March 1909.

44.   San Francisco Call, 4 July 1909.

45.   Examiner, 21 May 1909; Chronicle, 21 May 1909; Bulletin, 7 July 1909; Chronicle, 8 July 1909; Examiner, 8 July 1909; Labor Clarion, 23 July 1909; Chronicle, 8 August 1909; Irwin, "Adventures of Yesteryear," 308-309; Organized Labor, 24 July, 25 September 1909. Both the Labor Clarion and the Building Trades Council's weekly, Organized Labor, gave Local 48's effort coverage.

46.   Labor Clarion, 9 September, 20 August, 10 September 1909.

47.   Labor Clarion, 1 October, 3 December 1909.

48.   Sherry Katz, "Frances Noel and the Working Class Woman: Female Solidarity and Class Consciousness in Los Angeles, 1909-1916," (Seminar paper, University of California, Los Angeles, April 22, 1985), 3; Labor Clarion, 28 August, 1908; Katz, "Frances Noel," 3.

49.   Mead, "Trade Unionism and Political Activity Among San Francisco Wage-Earning Women, 1900-1922," 132-133. Labor Clarion, 12 February, 19 March, 21 May, 4 June, 11 June, 6 August, 5 February, 1909.

50.   Labor Clarion, 1 October, 19 November, 1909.

51.   Labor Clarion, 4 March, 11 March, 8 April, 21 January, 1 July, 8 July 1910.

52.   Labor Clarion, 5 August, 12 August 1910; San Francisco Labor Council papers, Folder "Laundry Workers' #26," Bancroft Library, University of California, Berkeley, CA.

53.   Labor Clarion, 2 September, 30 September, 7 October 1910.

54.   Labor Clarion, 28 October, 4 November, 14 November, 2 December, 30 December 1910; Organized Labor, 15 October 1910. While Louise LaRue is not listed as a WIULL activist, CESA Recording Secretary Jennie McBean noted that LaRue was scheduled to join Hannah Nolan in delivering the WUILL report at the CESA's 1909 state convention. Nolan arrived alone, stating that LaRue was ill. Jennie McBean, Carton 3, File "Notes, Minutes of Meetings, Ect. -Jennie V. McBean," Keith-Pond McHenry Papers, Bancroft Library, University of California, Berkeley, California.

55.   Katz, "Frances Noel," 3-4; Labor Clarion, 23 September 1910.

56.   Katz, "Frances Noel," 6; Labor Clarion, 25 February 1910.

57. Keith, "California in 1901-1920"; Solomons, How We Won the Vote in California, 16.

58. Eleanor Flexner, Century of Struggle (Cambridge: Belknap Press, 1959; New York: Atheneum, 1973), 254-255.

59. Rodes, "The California Woman Suffrage Campaign of 1911," 42-44. For a complete and classic account of the rise of Progressivism in California, see George E. Mowry, The California Progressives (Berkeley and Los Angeles: University of California Press, 1951).

60. Solomons, How We Won the Vote in California, 12; Rodes, "The California Woman Suffrage Campaign of 1911," 50; Chronicle, 19 January 1911; Examiner, 19 January 1911. For a more detailed account of the suffragists' lobbying effort on behalf of Amendment 8, see Rodes, "The California Woman Suffrage Campaign of 1911", 46-57.

61. Keith, California in 1901-1920; Labor Clarion, 24 February 1911; Call, 9 March 1911. Economist Lucile Eaves noted that only two California laws pertaining to women workers passed the legislature prior to 1910. The first prohibited women under 18 from working more than sixty hours per week, while a second mandated separate toilet facilities and seats for women workers during break periods. Both were enacted in 1889, but Eaves complained that neither law was well policed or enforced. She also notes that in two prior campaign for the eight-hour day for women workers, the California State Federation of Labor endorsed the proposed statute but did little lobbying on its behalf. The 1911 law, passed after Eaves completed her study, resulted mainly from the joint efforts of female reformers and women unionists. Lucile Eaves, A History of California Labor Legislation, pp. 225, 315-6. Interestingly, LaRue's testimony mirrored that of Elizabeth Mahony, secretary of Waitresses' Union Local 484 in Chicago when she testified in 1909 for an eight-hour law for Illinois women workers. When it appeared that the bill would not pass, supporters substituted a ten-hour measure which was enacted. Rheta Child Dorr, What Eight Million Women Want (Boston: Small, Maynard & Co., 1910), 158-164. For a more detailed account of the campaign for California's eight-hour law for women, see Earl C. Crockett, "History of California Labor Legislation, 1910-1930," Ph.D. dissertation, University of California, Berkeley, 1931.

62. Daily News, 2 March, 6 March 1911. Coffin probably took her position based on the compromise worked out in Illinois to substitute a ten-hour day bill for the eight-hour measure which seemed doomed to fail. In California, however, the ten-hour bill was proposed in opposition to the eight-hour version.

63.   Labor Clarion, 19 May 1911; Call, 14 June 1911.   One week later, LaRue also agreed to serve on the committee to organize the infamous annual ball for the sickness and death benefit fund. Call, 21 June 1911.

64.   Call, 12 July 1911; Labor Clarion, 14 July 1911.

65.   Labor Clarion, 21 July 1911; 18 August 1911.

66.   Harper, History of Woman Suffrage, 6:45; Call, 7 August 1911.

67.   Mabel Craft Deering, the Central Committee Chair, is credited with coordinating the production and distribution of campaign literature authorized by the Committee's constituent groups.   Rodes, " The California Woman Suffrage Campaign of 1911," 29; Maud Younger, "Why Working Women Should Vote," file "Clippings re Woman Suffrage 1911," carton 4, Keith-Pond-McHenry Papers.

68.   Call, 14 August 1911.

69.   Call, 7 August, 18 August 1911; Labor Clarion, 25 August 1911; Michael Kazin noted that the Brewery Workers had socialists in key positions of national leadership at this time, which might explain its prosuffrage stance.   Michael Kazin, "Barons of Labor: The San Francisco Building Trades, 1896-1922" (Ph.D. dissertation, Stanford University, 1983), 315.   The socialist weekly Revolt, edited by Tom Mooney, also listed two San Francisco brewery locals as "pioneer contributors" to the paper. Revolt, 6 May 1911.

70.   Call, 18 August 1911; San Francisco Daily News, 7 October 1911.

71.   Daily News, 17 August 1911.

72.   Daily News, 17 August 1911.

73.   Daily News, 17 August 1911.

74.   Daily News, 17 August 1911.

75.   Daily News, 17 August 1911.

76.   For another account of making the rounds of the San Francisco unions in the company of Maud Younger during this period, see Irwin, "Adventures of Yesteryear," 320-321.   Younger and Irwin sought labor's endorsement for a retrial of two organizers for the International Workers of the World (IWW) found guilty of murder at Wheatland in California's Central Valley.   Irwin later joined the National Women's Party with Younger and wrote a volume

commemorating the Party's history. Inez Haynes Irwin, "Up Hill With Banners Flying" (Penobscot, Maine: Traversity Press, 1964).

77.   Call, 24 August 1911; Chronicle, 24 August 1911; Call, 26 August 1911; Chronicle, 26 August 1911.

78.   Call, 31 August 1911; Daily News, 31 August, 1 September 1911; Examiner, 1 September 1911; Carole Hicke, "The 1911 Campaign of James Rolph, Jr., Mayor of All the People" (M.A. thesis, San Francisco State University, 1978), 36.   The September primary was San Francisco's first nonpartisan municipal election, established through a charter amendment in 1910. Issel and Cherny, San Francisco 1865-1932, 160.   McCarthy was a Johnny-come-lately to the suffrage cause, despite the long-standing support of women unionists such as LaRue.   Michael Kazin noted that McCarthy and the Building Trades Council endorsed Amendment Eight only a few months before the election, "a move probably calculated to win middle class progressives who tended to side with his opponent."   Kazin, "Barons of Labor," 585.

79.   Labor Clarion, 1 September 1911.

80.   Call, 5 September 1911; Chronicle, 5 September 1911; College Equal Suffrage League of Northern California, Winning Equal Suffrage in California (San Francisco: James H. Barry Co., 1913), 96-98.

81.   Call, 5 September 1911; Chronicle, 5 September 1911; College Equal Suffrage League of Northern California, Winning Equal Suffrage in California, 97-98.

82.   Call, 5 September 1911; Examiner, 5 September 1911; College Equal Suffrage League of Northern California, Winning Equal Suffrage in California, 97-98.

83.   Call, 5 September 1911; Examiner, 5 September 1911; Daily News, 5 September 1911; College Equal Suffrage League, Winning Equal Suffrage in California, 97

84.   Labor Clarion, 6 October 1911; Call, 6 October 1911; Call, 7 October 1911; Examiner, 7 October 1911; Daily News, 7 October 1911.

85.   San Francisco, Board of Supervisors, San Francisco Municipal Reports for the Fiscal Year 1911-1912 Ending June 30, 1912 (San Francisco: Neal Publishing Co., 1913), 231.   While it is assumed that suffrage carried in southern California due to its Protestant, progressive character, this has not been tested and is still a matter of speculation.

86.   Frank C. Jordan, Secretary of State, Statement of the Vote of California at the Special Election Held October 10, 1911 on Constitutional Amendments (Sacramento: Superintendent of State Printing, 1911), 4. Mary McHenry Keith, "Political Situation," Keith- Pond-McHenry Papers, File "Woman Suffrage Campaign in California," Bancroft Library, Berkeley, California.   There is evidence to indicate that Keith accurately perceived ambivalence by male Progressives toward the suffrage issue. Amendment Eight did not appear on the list of "preferred amendments" published by the California Republican Party. Indeed, Governor Hiram Johnson held the suffrage cause at arm's length. Historian George Mowry characterized Johnson as "emotionally opposed to women in politics."   When asked, during a military parade review at the Presidio, whether he was "with" the suffragists, he replied, "This is where the army retreats."   George Mowry, The California Progressives (Berkeley: University of California Press, 1951), 148; Keith, "California in 1901-1920;" Alan P. Grimes, The Puritan Ethic and Woman Suffrage (New York: Oxford University Press, 1967), 101. Philip Ethington believes that gender conflict lay at the heart of the progressive desire to redefine the public sphere, and uses San Francisco's voting data during the 1911 vote for woman suffrage as a case study. He concludes that "feminist support for Progressivism was not matched with Progressive support for feminism. . . The majority of urban men simply refused to accept female partnership in the Progressive-era reconstruction of the municipal household." Philip J. Ethington, "Gender, Class, and Privilege: The Contested Terrain of Political Culture in San Francisco, 1890-1920," paper presented at the American Historical Association annual meeting, 27-30 December 1989.

87.   George E. Mowry, The California Progressives (Chicago: Quadrangle Books, 1963), 149; Grimes, The Puritan Ethic and Woman Suffrage, 106.

88.   William Issel and Robert W. Cherny, San Francisco 1865-1932, (Berkeley and Los Angeles: University of California Press, 1986), 58, 63-66; San Francisco, Board of Supervisors, Municipal Reports , 231.

89.   San Francisco, Board of Supervisors, Municipal Reports, 1911-1912, 231. Jules Tygiel, " 'Where Unionism Holds Undisputed Sway' -- A Reappraisal of San Francisco's Union Labor Party," California History 62 (Fall 1983): 207.

90.   Issel and Cherny, San Francisco 1865-1932, 58, 75-76; San Francisco, Board of Supervisors, Municipal Reports, 1911-1912, 231.

91.   San Francisco, Board of Supervisors, Municipal Reports, 1911-1912, 231; Issel and Cherny, San Francisco 1865-1932, 68-75.

92.   Mary McHenry Keith, "Archbishop Riordan on Woman Suffrage," File "Clippings re Woman Suffrage, 1911," Carton 4, Keith-Pond-McHenry Papers.

93.   The Leader, 1 April 1911, 4 February 1911. Interestingly, Father Yorke espoused a pro-suffrage position shortly before the 1896 campaign. As editor of The Monitor, the newspaper of the San Francisco Archdiocese, he argued that women voters represented the last hope for the salvation of American cities. "Men are not as awake to the evils which flourish in our midst as women are. . . . Nature has centered them in the home and they will judge of men and measure by the standard of the home," he maintained. Yorke also asserted that the average American woman was intellectually superior to men and would apply Christianity to public life with greater diligence than men. These words stand in strong contrast to Yorke's perspective on the woman's vote fifteen years later and it is not clear why Yorke switched camps. The Monitor, 9 March 1895.

94.   While Yorke vociferously attacked woman suffrage in the pages of The Leader during the 1911 campaign, other local Catholic clergymen gave overt or tacit support to the suffrage cause. Father Joseph Gleason of Palo Alto addressed a pro-suffrage audience at San Francisco's Central Theatre in May 1911, where he proclaimed, "You know as well as I do that a woman is just as fit to vote as a man." Archbishop Patrick W. Riordan took an extremely understated public position. Speaking at Oakland's MacDonough Theater, he hedged making an unqualified endorsement by saying only that he had not "read a single argument against it that was worth considering." Despite this seemingly weak stand, suffragists honored Riordan upon his death in 1915. They praising the aforementioned speech as well as an edict Riordan issued in 1911 which ordered that parish priests remain silent on the issue of suffrage. Riordan also wrote a circular letter in 1912 urging Catholic women to register and vote. In doing so, they would exercise "the chiefest of civic obligations." This letter was read in every parish church. An article with similar sentiments appeared in The Monitor, the San Francisco Archdiocese's weekly newspaper. Catholic Church leaders, then, articulated a range of views on women's enfranchisement. As "labor's priest," however, Yorke's convictions probably carried more weight among working-class parishioners. "Extracts from the speech of the Rev. Father Gleason at Central Theatre San Francisco, May 23, 1911," File "Clippings re Woman Suffrage 1911," Carton 4, Keith-Pond McHenry Papers; Mary McHenry Keith, "Archbishop Riordan on Woman Suffrage," Keith-Pond-McHenry Papers; California Equal Suffrage Association, "In Memoriam: His Grace the Most Reverend Patrick William Riordan, Archbishop of San Francisco," Chancery Archives, San Francisco Archdiocese, Colma, California; Circular letter, 8 August 1912; Circular Letters, Oct. 1908-Oct. 1931, Chancery Archives; The Monitor, 27 January 1912.

95.   Helen Valeska Bary, "Labor Administration and Social Security: A Woman's Life," oral history, 1974, Regional Oral History Project, Bancroft Library, University of California, Berkeley, California, 23-24.

96.   Harper, History of Woman Suffrage, 6:46.

97.   Michael Kazin, Barons of Labor, 184; San Francisco Examiner 3 September 1911

98.   Keith, "California in 1901-1920." Saloon keepers and the manufacturers of alcoholic beverages had good reason to fear women's votes. The Anti-Saloon League's pro-suffrage stance in 1911 provided only one reason for anti-prohibitionists to renew their campaign against female enfranchisement. An explosion of temperance victories in Northern California, as well as in the south of the state, took place between 1909 and 1913. Hundreds of towns and supervisorial districts voted to go "dry", with many of those contests taking place after the 1911 woman suffrage victory. Gilman M. Ostrander, The Prohibition Movement in California, 1846-1933, University of California Publications in History, vol. 57 (Berkeley and Los Angeles: University of California Press, 1957), 116-117.

99.   Labor Clarion, 20 October 1911.

AFTERMATH AND CONCLUSIONS

"THIS NEWER AND LARGER WOMAN'S MOVEMENT"

1911 saw the beginning of a political realignment in San Francisco and its decline as a "union town." In the same year that California women won the vote, labor lost its control over San Francisco city government as the Union Labor Party was voted out of office. Campaigning as the candidate "for all the people," James Rolph, Jr., handily won the mayoral race, capturing 47,427 votes to McCarthy's 27,067. The elimination of partisan elections by progressives eager to separate the ULP from its working-class identity and popularity partially explains the defeat.[1] While it retained a few seats on the Board of Supervisors, Union Labor Party political dominance quickly became a memory as Rolph and progressive Republicans moved into the forefront. Most unionists eventually became active in the Republican Party.[2]

Organizations devoted to woman suffrage typically died or were transformed into tools of progressivism. The College Equal Suffrage League became the Civic League of California, the predecessor of the California League of Women Voters. The Clubwomen's Franchise League transformed itself into the New Era Club, which carried out voter registration drives for clubwomen.

Selina Solomons's Votes for Women Club gave itself a grand "funeral" and its membership dispersed.[3]

What became of the Wage Earner's League?   The Labor Clarion continued to list it as an official labor organization through May 1912. By the time it disappeared from the Labor Council's roster, the organization's activists had trained their sights on another objective--registering working-class women to vote. The women of San Francisco had their first chance to cast their ballots on March 28, 1912, when the city considered a bond issue to fund the construction of a grand new Civic Center and replace municipal buildings destroyed by the earthquake. Apparently the numbers of women registering to vote in the working-class districts fell far below the numbers of women in the middle-class and wealthy areas of San Francisco. Concerned by this gap, a special committee of the San Francisco Labor Council met with members of the San Francisco WIULL on March 21, 1912 at the Council's offices. WIULL representatives included Minna O'Donnell, Hannah Nolan, a Mrs. Carson of the Laundry Workers' Union, and Maud Younger.[4]

The Labor Council delegates agreed with the WIULL about the "absolute necessity of organizing the women voters of the State, or, at least, awakening them to a form of organization conducive to the furtherance of humane legislation and the work of organized labor bodies." To that end, the joint body proposed that, beginning with San Francisco, the labor community bring together "the wives and relatives of Trade Unionists and sympathizers with the cause and [weld] them into permanent organizations." The movement would then spread outward to "the different towns in the State of California," coordinated by a main office in San Francisco. To further this end, the joint body requested that the Labor Council allocate $500 towards the effort's expenses and hire a woman organizer to carry out the group's goals.[5]

The following evening, the Labor Council affirmed the report of the joint body. One week later, the Labor Clarion printed a front-page plea to its readers.

To the men, it pronounced that "it is the duty of the men of the labor movement to urge upon the female members of their families the advantages to be gained by registering at once and by affiliating with the clubs to be organized by the Women's Union Label League in each Assembly District." The Clarion in turn spoke to women, saying, "Every working women, every housewife in a working family, every woman who has at heart the best interests of her kind should associate herself with one of these clubs at as early a date as possible. . . .Work is the thing. Get in and do your part now."[6]

The joint committee met again on April 9, 1912. The body reported that the new organization would be known as the Women's Humane Legislation League. It also called for the formation of a governing board composed of women from various Labor Council affiliates, delegates of the Building Trades Council, and members of the WIULL.[7]

The Humane Legislation League did not begin to function officially until early June, when hired organizer Frances Noel left her home in Los Angeles to assume her duties in San Francisco. Noel, a socialist active in the Los Angeles WIULL, had organized the Los Angeles chapter of the Wage Earners' Suffrage League. Noel directly contacted sympathetic women unionists and the female relatives of male unionists. These women, she reported, circulated a leaflet entitled "Woman's Appeal to Women"; they circulated it door-to-door, at factory gates, and on the street urging women to "REGISTER IN TIME. BE A VOTER. VOTE FOR JUSTICE TO WORKERS AND THE PROTECTION OF THE RACE." It also entreated women to help with the work of the Humane Legislation League. In particular, the Humane Legislation League targeted the preservation of the eight-hour day for women, then being challenged in the courts. At the end of her tenure as the League's organizer, Noel claimed that "the registration of women in the Labor districts appears, thus far, proportionately as high as it is in the other districts. Thus we can feel that our efforts have brought results."[8]

Noel's estimate of the results was partially correct. By 1913, San Francisco women living in working-class neighborhoods had registered in impressive numbers. Most women registrants lived in the city's artisanal district, with women in the middle-class Richmond-Fillmore area bringing up a close second place (Table 17). When comparing the women registered in the various neighborhoods to the total number of women residing there, however, it is clear that the middle-class and upper-class areas surpassed the pro-labor districts in the proportion of women registrants per neighborhood. The ratio of registrants to the total number of women was greater in neighborhoods housing residents of a higher socioeconomic class. While the Humane Legislation League may have increased the number of working-class-class women voters, the proportion of women registrants in the other districts remained higher (Table 18).

If the campaign to register working-class women for the vote brought results in terms of new female voters, it also served to show that the labor community at large was less than committed when asked to transfer its support for an abstract constitutional right to encouraging their sisters, wives, and daughters to cast a ballot. In her final report, Noel complained that the constituent unions of the San Francisco Labor Council were of little help during the registration effort. While reiterating that she believed that "organized labor stands for the highest and the best," she also rebuked the Labor Council affiliates for their disinterest. "Men of San Francisco, you have taken a rather conservative stand toward this newer and larger woman's movement," she charged. In concluding, Noel hoped that, in the interest of labor's advancement, male unions and unionists "and the woman's movement would join hands on the battleground of the world's emancipation toward a higher standard of human life." Like progressive-minded men, perhaps San Francisco union men lacked enthusiasm when asked to share the role of municipal decision-making with women.[9]

TABLE 17

SAN FRANCISCO FEMALE VOTING REGISTRATION, FY 1912-1912

Neighborhood	Assembly Districts	Number of Women Registered	Total SF Citizens Registered
South-of-Market	21-24*	8963 (18.0%)	33,711 (23.0%)
Artisanal	25,26,29	14,392 (28.9%)	41,271 (28.2%)
Fillmore-Richmond	27,28,30	14247 (28.6%)	37,594 (25.7%)
Pacific Heights	31	5271 (10.6%)	12,259 (8.3$)
Downtown-Marina	32	5327 (10.7%)	13,613 ((9.3%)
Waterfront	33	1633 (3.3%)	8014 (5.5%)
TOTAL		49,833 (100%)	146,462 (100%)

*Redistricted 1912

Source: San Francisco, Board of Supervisors, <u>San Francisco Municipal Reports, 1913-1914</u> (San Francisco: Neal Publishing Co., 1915), 274.

TABLE 18

COMPARISON OF FEMALE REGISTRATION TO FEMALE POPULATION
IN SAN FRANCISCO BY NEIGHBORHOOD, FY 1912-1913

Neighborhood	% of Women Registered by Neighborhood	% of Women Residents in Neighborhoods	Ratio of Registration to Population
South-of-Market	26.6%	38.8%	.69
Artisanal	34.9%	47.4%	.74
Fillmore-Richmond	37.9%	48.1%	.79
Pacific Heights	43.0%	50.8%	.85
Downtown-Marina	39.1%	45.4%	.86
Waterfront	20.4%	27.4%	.74

Sources: San Francisco, Board of Supervisors, Municipal Reports, 1913-1914, 274; U.S. Bureau of the Census, Thirteenth Census of the United States: 1910, Abstract of the Census with Supplement for California, 616.

The San Francisco WIULL survived until 1913, when the San Francisco Labor Council merged the group with its Union Label Section and diminished the San Francisco WIULL to auxiliary status in exchange for financial support. Never a large organization, the leadership was able to muster little interest among other women unionists to attend meetings. When the organization lost its autonomy and ability to function independently from the Council, even the die-hard members drifted away and it disintegrated. A Ladies Auxiliary of the Label Section reappeared in 1922, apparently sparked into existence by a threatened decrease in the minimum wage, but no sustained group resulted.[10]

Tensions between female reformers and wage-earning women lingered after 1911, causing further ill will and distrust. In 1913, San Francisco clubwomen succeeded in closing the dance halls of the Barbary Coast. Suffragists Mary Sperry and Elizabeth Gerberding were among the reformers who called for a "a clean city for clean people" through the closure of the seamy quarter's dance halls. This action left approximately 400 to 600 women formerly employed in the dance halls destitute, unable to support either themselves or dependent children and elderly parents who relied on their income. The reformers added insult to injury when they urged the "dance hall girls" to seek "respectable" work. The reformers chiefly wrote off the dancers as hopelessly immoral creatures who were the prisoners of their own sensuality and limited mentality. For their part, most of the dancers rejected what little help the clubwomen offered, refusing the maternal brand of attention they extended. Some returned to work in other dancing establishments. To add insult to injury, some clubwomen declined to walk a picket line during a cloakmaker's strike because of their preoccupation with the elimination of vice.[11]

That same year, female reformers promoted legislation for a minimum wage for female wage-earners. In addition to ensuring that women workers be paid an adequate wage, the reformers argued that a living wage would prevent working-class women from falling victim to white slavery or voluntarily exchanging their virtue for gifts, entertainment and money, due to their lower moral standards. Progressive legislators echoed these views during debates held on the Assembly and Senate floors of the California legislature on the minimum wage for women. The San Francisco Labor Council opposed the measure, fearing that it would impede organizing female wage-earners, institutionalize governmental intervention in the collective bargaining process and set a wage ceiling for women that employers would refuse to go beyond.[12]

Female unionists on the Council led the way on this issue and were responsible for the Council's position. They especially objected to the inferences reformers made regarding the alleged moral standards of wage-earning women. Sarah Hagan, president of the United Garment Workers Union Local #131, denounced such a presumption when addressing the state legislature on the proposed bill and advised the body that union organizations would do more for women workers than a minimum wage. Despite Hagan's testimony and that of other unionists, the measure passed handily. The Industrial Welfare Commission (IWC), which administered and monitored the minimum wage law, and its reform advocates continued to be the targets of the union women's resentment. Hagan withheld wage rate information from the Commission during a 1914 investigation. Almost a decade later, in 1922, she publicly debated Los Angeles reformer and IWC Executive Commissioner Katherine Edson regarding the IWC's work and, specifically, its attempt at that time to lower the minimum wage for women from $16.00 to $15.00 per week. Hagan, the San Francisco Labor Council and the California Federation of Labor persevered in expressing their antagonism against the IWC throughout the 1920s.[13]

In both cases, middle-class reformers assumed a patronizing posture toward working-class women. They presumed to act in loco parentis based on their notion of morality, their desire to protect wage-earning women from their own ignorance and passions, and their belief in their entitlement to perform such a role. Female wage-earners responded with indignation, rejecting the role of girls and daughters that "city mothers" espoused. Women unionists shared this sense of outrage and articulated a defense of female wage-earners's morality and the idea of class self-help. Clearly the two bands of activists remained polar opposites, at least in their own eyes.

In the years following, Maud Younger continued her participation in union women's causes such as a International Ladies Garment Workers Union boycott against white goods, or underwear and negligees during a 1913 New York strike. That same year, Younger urged San Francisco union locals to endorse a new trial for two members of the International Workers of the World convicted of murder while organizing migrant farm labor in Wheatland, California. According to Alice Paul, she also financed the legal defense of the Eight-Hour Day Law for Women in the California court system and before the United States Supreme Court. The Supreme Court sustained the law in February 1915, winning Younger the accolade "Mother of the Eight Hour Day for Women." She also returned to suffrage work when she signed on to stump for the cause again during the 1914 state campaign in Nevada. While campaigning, she refused to patronize hotels boycotted by the labor movement.[14]

Younger's full attention turned to suffrage, however, after a portentous meeting with Alice Paul at the Panama Pacific International Exposition in San Francisco in 1915. Paul headed up the Congressional Union, a suffrage organization which favored militant demonstrations in support of the right to vote, such as outdoor rallies, marches and picketing. The group considered itself the American equivalent of the British suffragettes of the Women's Social and Political Union, which fire-bombed mailboxes, broke windows and carried out hunger strikes after being imprisoned. Paul persuaded Younger to join the fledgling organization. Thereafter, Younger divided her time between the San Francisco Bay Area and Congressional Union headquarters in Washington, D.C.[15]

Younger did not spell out her reasons for shifting her main commitment from labor organizing to suffrage. Inez Haynes Irwin claimed that Younger had

simply come to the realization that unions were "not the whole answer" and
decided to dedicate her energy to suffrage as a remedy for female worker's
problems.[16]

The basis for this vague justification becomes clearer in light of an
emerging spirit of frustration and dissatisfaction among New York NWTUL
women committed to unionization during this period. Long-time activists such
as Rose Schneiderman, Pauline Newman, Melinda Scott and Leonora O'Reilly
felt forsaken both by the AFL, which displayed a half-hearted enthusiasm for
unionizing women, and by their reform-minded counterparts in the organization,
who leaned increasingly towards legislative solutions for the obstacles wage-
earning women faced. Newman and Schneiderman left the NWTUL temporarily
in 1914 to organize for the International Ladies Garment Workers' Union, but
returned several years later after clashes with male union officials. Scott and
O'Reilly quit permanently shortly afterward.   While Scott returned to her
organizing post with the United Garment Worker's Union, O'Reilly abandoned
labor movement activity altogether.[17]

Younger painted a rosy picture of her relationship with the San Francisco
labor movement in her autobiography. Yet, Frances Noel's observations on
labor's indifference to women's concerns indicated that antagonism existed
between the male-dominated labor movement and union feminists. It is possible
that a similar sense of futility infected Younger during these years and caused her
to look beyond organized labor for the means to bring justice to female wage-
earners.

Eleanor Flexner described Younger as Alice Paul's lieutenant during the
campaign for the federal woman suffrage amendment, commencing in 1916.
That same year, the group changed its name to the National Women's Party
(NWP), which it retains to this day. Younger's final years were spent pursuing
the passage of the Equal Rights Amendment (ERA), authored by Paul and
promoted by the NWP. Based on its belief in absolute legal equality and its

advocacy of the ERA, the NWP condemned all gender-based labor legislation after 1923. Ironically, the "Mother of the Eight Hour Day for Women" turned her back on protective legislation to support the ERA. According to Younger, laws protecting only female wage-earner served "to lower women's economic status, keep them in the ranks with little chance for advancement . . . and to perpetuate the psychology that they are cheap labor and inferior to other adult workers." What was needed, Younger suggested, was "industrial equality," a concept she believed the NRA legislation of the New Deal promoted. The ERA, she felt, would carry this equality into the nonworking aspects of women's lives. In taking this position, Younger in effect severed her relationship with organized labor. She articulated the pain this caused her in her autobiography, but concluded that, "Nevertheless one had to choose; the choice must be made." Based on its stance on protective labor legislation, the NWP opposed a 1927 extension of the California Eight-Hour Day Law for Women, repudiating the legislation for which Younger proudly took credit. The measure was defeated due, in part, to the NWP's effort. Younger died in 1936 at her ranch in Los Gatos, California.[18]

Little is known about the subsequent careers of women such as Minna O'Donnell or Louise LaRue. As with most working-class women, their history can only be substantiated as individuals when it intersects with widely publicized and documented movements and people, rather than documented through archival searches for personal papers. They did not write articles for the daily press or publish articles in national magazines about their exploits in the labor and suffrage movements. Nothing is known of O'Donnell beyond her connection with the Humane Legislation League. LaRue continued to act as a Labor Council delegate for Local 48. A 1912 Chronicle article revealed that she was a member of the executive board of the California Civic League. LaRue continued to hold membership in the Civic League in 1922, which had by then affiliated with the League of Women Voters.[19]

The San Francisco Wage Earner's Suffrage League's history, however, demonstrates that union women participated fully and vigorously in the California woman suffrage movement's last state campaign for enfranchisement. Through involvement in the WESL, these women lobbied the men and women of their own community on the cause of suffrage in union meetings, on public platforms, and in the streets. They worked on their own, but also they joined with mainstream suffragists in forming a coalition that blanketed the state with pro-suffrage literature.

The WESL drew its leadership from San Francisco's largely Irish female work force. These independent white women, who married later than average and lived away from their immediate families in significant numbers, tended to invest in their identity as wage-earners and view themselves as potentially life-long workers. They unionized at a higher rate than did women nationally due to a more receptive labor community, the presence of a unifying anti-Asian movement, the opportunity to form separate women's unions, and their ability to generate a contingent of capable union leaders. These women participated fully in San Francisco's union structures. In addition to leading their own locals, they represented those unions on the San Francisco Labor Council and participated in the California Federation of Labor. Inspired by the power the labor community wielded in municipal politics, by their own ability to generate a layer of union leadership and by the stimulus provided by a revitalized woman suffrage movement, they became adherents to the suffrage cause.

These autonomous women's union locals, with Waitresses' Local 48 in particular, were a combination working-class women's club, benevolent society and agent of social change. They provided the environment which nurtured the development of female union leadership and allowed these unionists to define and pursue issues of special interest to their female membership. They also provided the vehicles for the involvement of this leadership in municipal politics and in the campaign for woman suffrage.

Unionists founded the WESL after they discovered they could not coexist with mainstream suffragists in one organization, the San Francisco Equal Suffrage League. Their middle-class sisters' unwillingness to support a critical strike, combined with differences over temperance, moral reform, and the San Francisco graft prosecution, drove them from the organization and eventually resulted in the formation of the WESL in 1908. Waitresses' Local 48, its representative Louise LaRue, and Minna O'Donnell of the Typographical Union's Auxiliary stood at the heart of the group. Maud Younger, an upper-middle class women with labor sympathies, assisted with the WESL's founding and helped sustain the organization through the 1911 campaign.

It is also clear that the WESL and its successor, the HLL, were self-consciously white. While women like Louise LaRue campaigned to exclude Asians and other racial minorities from the union, the craft and, indeed, the nation, spokeswomen Noel and Younger appealed for support for female enfranchisement as a "protection of the race," and the white women who had born and raised children, "mothers of the race." These suggestions of racial endangerment and assumptions of white solidarity punctuated calls for woman suffrage and for the necessity of white female political participation.

The WESL was not a large, grass-roots organization which emphasized membership recruitment. Most of the League's recorded activists were a small core of union leaders who had a proven track record of commitment to the concerns of wage-earning women. Motivated by the vision of working-class women's involvement in municipal affairs and their own empowerment, women such as LaRue and O'Donnell initiated a series of organizations. In addition to the Wage Earners' Suffrage League, they organized the Twentieth Century Club and reactivated a local chapter of the WIULL in order to build interest in the issues and concerns women working outside the home encountered, and also to generate a measure of political and social clout for themselves. These groups also sustained a level of visibility and activity between campaigns for woman suffrage. During the 1911 campaign, woman suffrage supplanted most of the focus of their activity.

Nevertheless, union business, their involvement in the Labor Council and family life may have infringed on their abilities to be full-time suffragists and political activists. Maud Younger, on the other hand, was a relatively free agent. A financially independent, pro-union suffragist, she provided critical support and resources to the WESL. She had the time to concern herself with organizational detail and functioning; enough time to take on responsibilities in Local 48 as well as in the WESL and the other organizations. Women such as Younger, her southern counterpart Frances Noel, and Harriot Stanton Blatch proved to be invaluable partners for their working-class sisters.[20]

Because Younger believed that unionization was the primary tool for workplace change for women, she propounded an alternative view to that of the majority of suffragists who held the vote to be the ultimate emancipator for all women.   Younger's beliefs were far more compatible with those of union suffragists and the labor community in general. Because of this, and her possession of a union card, she seemed to be taken into the labor community as one of its own.

Maud Younger came to be an ally of working-class suffragists through a personal transformation that began in the days of her settlement house work and her growing dissatisfaction with benevolence and reform. Fueled by the transference of her loyalty to the National Women's Trade Union League and her experience as a waitress, Younger forged a new identity that combined her new-found competence as a wage-earner and her desire for social change. In San Francisco, her sensibility, reflecting this new consciousness, was galvanized by her new association with Local 48. She became a part of the labor community, albeit a idiosyncratic and unique one, acting out her desire to speak with, not for wage-earning women. She provided a bridge between union suffragists and their reform-minded counterparts, identifying with the first and sharing the social and family status of the second.

Her relationship with the women of the WESL was that of an equal and colleague, especially with regard to Louise LaRue. Younger passed on LaRue's advice on organizing the labor community for suffrage, made the rounds of union halls with her to secure endorsements for Amendment 8, and eventually travelled the state with her as labor's representatives for women's right to vote. Women like LaRue won Younger's admiration and the feeling appeared mutual.

Particularly when addressing working-class audiences, Younger made a point of referring to herself as a wage-earner and union woman. Given Younger's visage, her activities, and her reputation as a "millionaire waitress" were well publicized, those listening probably knew her background and her actual class status. Certainly Younger never spurned her family, relinquished her independent income, or renounced the privileges of her class. Her allusions to being a worker and a unionist represented an act of solidarity with the working class, and especially with wage-earning women.[21]

Her short stint as a waitress initiated her into labor; her enduring commitment to Local 48 and her use of labor rhetoric secured her a more permanent place in the community. This connection lasted until she acted to sever the relationship with her support for the Equal Rights Amendment in the 1920s.

The WESL transformed the labor community's pro-suffrage sentiment into concrete support and mobilized San Francisco union leaders on behalf of the suffrage campaign. WESL activists secured endorsements as credentialed Labor Council representatives, sponsored meetings that featured Labor Council and Union Labor Party leaders as speakers, and directly addressed their union brothers in the pages of the Labor Clarion. Voting data suggest that the WESL's activity together with union endorsements influenced a significant number of voters in the working class districts to support Amendment Eight. The percentage of pro-suffrage votes in working-class districts rose significantly from those cast in 1896. Indeed, it could be argued that, in the narrow statewide victory, this block of votes may have made the difference between defeat and passage for Amendment Eight.[22]

While San Francisco unions and their rank-and-file members could favor woman suffrage in the abstract, it appears that these same men shied away from implementing it when it came to their own families, as the experience with the Humane Legislation League demonstrated. This body, however, demonstrated that union suffragists continued to be active and successfully promoted the registration of women in working-class districts.

Finally, the WESL broadened the perspective of the suffrage movement and helped to expand outreach to women of other economic backgrounds and cultures. It was not until after the formation of the League that the College Equal Suffrage League opened its membership to include wage-earners and Selina Solomons formed the Votes for Women Club. Its existence contributed to the growing recognition of working-class support for suffrage. The WESL soon inspired the formation of other chapters in Los Angeles, New York City, and Chicago.[23]

Histories that neglect to credit organizations such as the WESL or working-class feminists such as LaRue and O'Donnell deny by omission the breadth of movements organized around women's issues and their potential to politicize women across class lines, as well as how this becomes a reality. Through the development of autonomous organizations such as the WESL, suffrage reached a greater audience and had an increased chance of broad acceptance and support. While Amendment Eight failed in San Francisco in 1911, the Wage Earners' Suffrage League activity helped widen the debate on women's role and enlisted working-class women to carry their own banner in the march towards universal woman suffrage in the United States.

NOTES TO AFTERMATH AND CONCLUSION

1.   Carole Hicke, "The 1911 Campaign of James Rolph, Jr., Mayor of All the People" (M.A. thesis, San Francisco State University, 1978), 62; Michael Kazin, Barons of Labor: The San Francisco Building Trades and Union Power in the Progressive Era (Urbana and Chicago: University of Illinois Press, 1987), 196. Hicke also documents the rise of a new politics of personality. Rolph's campaign stressed his belief in nonpartisanship through a multi-partisan spectrum of support and underscored his "sunny" disposition. Publicity contrasted his philosophy of unity and his congenial demeanor with McCarthy's connections with disreputable figures, his identification as labor's candidate and his lack of personal charm. The affable Rolph claimed that his harmonious administration would represent the interests of all San Franciscans. A product of the Mission district, Rolph projected himself as someone at home in any neighborhood.

2.   William Issel and Robert W. Cherny, San Francisco, 1865-1932: Politics, Power and Urban Development (Berkeley and Los Angeles: University of California, 1986), 45-46; Jules Tygiel, " 'Where Unionism Holds Undisputed Sway' -- A Reappraisal of San Francisco's Union Labor Party," California History 62 (Fall 1983): 213. For an informative article on working-class voting behavior after 1911, see Thomas R. Clark, "Labor and Progressivism 'South of the Slot': The Voting Behavior of the San Francisco Working Class, 1912-1916," California History 66 (September 1987): 196-207, 234-236.

3.   Selina Solomons, How We Won the Vote in California: A True Story of the Campaign of 1911 (San Francisco: The New Woman Publishing Co., n.d.), 67-68.

4.   Chronicle, 28 March 1912; Untitled Report, San Francisco Labor Council Papers, carton 22, folder "Women's Trade Union League", Bancroft Library, Berkeley, CA. It is also probable that the Civic Center Bond issue offered little attraction to potential working-class women voters and they therefore had no incentive to register to vote on this particular measure. Unfortunately, no aggregate data on female voter registration in San Francisco is available before the 1912 general election in November. It is, therefore, not possible to state how great a gap existed between the numbers of working-class women registering to vote in comparison with their middle-class and wealthy counterparts.

5.   Untitled Report, San Francisco Labor Council Papers, folder "Women's Trade Union League," Bancroft Library, University of California, Berkeley, California.

6.   Labor Clarion, 29 March 1912.

7.   "To the Officers and Delegates of the San Francisco Labor Council," San Francisco Labor Council papers, folder "Women's Trade Union League."

8.   Labor Clarion, 9 August 1912; Sherry Katz, "Frances Nacke Noel and 'Sister Movements': Socialism, Feminism and Trade Unionism in Los Angeles, 1909-1916," California History 67 (September 1988), 182-184; Frances Noel Papers, Box 1, folder 8, Special Collections Department, University Research Library, University of California, Los Angeles; Labor Clarion, 9 August 1912. Noel's reference to "the protection of the race" probably reflects the continuing campaign to force Asian labor out of the labor market and to extend the Asian Exclusion Act to all Asians.

9.   Labor Clarion, 9 August 1912; Rebecca Mead, "Trade Unionism and Political Activity Among San Francisco Wage-Earning Women, 1900-1922" (Master's thesis, San Francisco State University, 1991), 125-126. Indeed, Maud Younger reported that while female wage-earners had either registered or declared the intent to do so, housewives generally refused to register to vote. It seemed that women who worked outside the home felt freer to exercise their right to vote than homemakers. San Francisco Daily News, 30 July 1912.

10.   Mead, "Trade Unionism and Political Activity Among San Francisco Wage-Earning Women, 1900-1922," 137, 196.

11.   Gayle Gullett, "City Mothers, City Daughters, and the Dance Hall Girls: The Limits of Female Political Power in San Francisco, 1913," in Women and the Structure of Society: Selected Research from the Fifth Berkshire Conference on the History of Women, ed. Barbara J. Harris and JoAnn K. McNamara (Durham. N.C.: Duke University Press, 1984), 149-159; Mead, "Trade Unionism and Political Activity Among San Francisco Wage-Earning Women, 1900-1922," 161-163, 93.

12.   Mead, "Trade Unionism and Political Activity Among San Francisco Wage-Earning Women, 1900-1922," 167-173.

13.   Mead, "Trade Unionism and Political Activity Among San Francisco Wage-Earning Women, 1900-1922," 174-209.

14.   Eleanor Flexner, "Maud Younger" in Edward T. James, Janet Wilson James and Paul S. Boyer, ed. Notable American Women 1607-1950, vol. 3 (Cambridge: Belknap Press, 1971), 700; Vera Edmundson, "Feminist and Laborite," Sunset Magazine (June 1915): 1180; Maud Younger, "Along the Way - Strike and Jail," National Women's Party Papers: Part II, Containers 195-196,

Library of Congress, Washington, D.C.; Inez Haynes Irwin, "Adventures of Yesteryear", Inez H. Irwin papers, Schlesinger Library, Radcliffe College, Cambridge, Mass., 320-321; Alice Paul, "Conversations with Alice Paul: Woman Suffrage and the Equal Rights Amendment," oral history conducted by Amelia Fry, Suffrage Oral History Project of the Regional Oral History Project, Bancroft Library, University of California, Berkeley, California, 1976; Examiner, 24 February 1915; letter, Maud Younger to Ann Martin, 28 September, 1914, Ann Martin Papers, Part I, Box 7, folder "Maud Younger", Bancroft Library, Berkeley, California. See Philip Foner, Women and the American Labor Movement (New York: The Free Press, 1979), 368-373 for a account of the 1913 White Goods Strike. For a more detailed account of the Wheatland riot and the subsequent conviction of "Blackie" Ford and Herman Suhr, see Hyman Weintraub, "The IWW in California: 1905-1931" (M.A. Thesis, University of California, Los Angeles, 1947), 68-84 and David Vaught, "Wheatland, The Press, and California Progressivism" (M.A. thesis, San Francisco State University, 1990). Inez Haynes Irwin accompanied Younger on her rounds of the unions on behalf of Ford and Suhr. She later joined the National Women's Party with Younger and wrote a volume commemorating the Party's history. Inez Haynes Irwin, Up Hill With Banners Flying (Penobscot, Maine: Traversity Press, 1964).

15.   Alice Paul, "Conversations with Alice Paul, 293, 430-31. Ellen Carol DuBois postulates that the militance of the organizations such as the Congressional Union and, later, the National Women's Party represented not only an imitation of the British suffragette's tactics but was also "an import from the labor movement." She explains, "The developments that were broadening the class basis and the outlook of American suffragism had prepared American women to respond to the heroism of the British militants." Younger may have also made this connection, which could have influenced her decision to take up the cudgel for suffrage as a member of the NWP. Ellen DuBois, "Working Women, Class Relations and Suffrage Militance: Harriot Stanton Blatch and the New York Woman Suffrage Movement, 1894-1909," Journal of American History 74 (June 1987): 52. For more detailed examinations of the National Women's Party, see Christine Lunardini, From Equal Suffrage to Equal Rights: Alice Paul and the National Women's Party, 1913-1928 (New York: New York University Press, 1986) and Susan D. Becker, The Origins of the Equal Rights Amendment: American Feminism Between the Wars (Westport, Conn.: Greenwood Press, 1981).

16.   Irwin, "Adventures of Yesteryear," 309.

17.   Foner, Women and the American Labor Movement, 318-323; Nancy Schrom Dye, As Equals and As Sisters (Columbia: University of Missouri

Press), 118-121; Alice Kessler-Harris, Out To Work (New York and Oxford: Oxford University Press, 1982), 155-166.

18.   Eleanor Flexner, Century of Struggle (Cambridge: Harvard University Press, 1959; New York: Atheneum, 1973), 280-293; Flexner, "Maud Younger," 700; Maud Younger, "The NRA and Protective Laws for Women," Literary Digest 117 (2 June 2 1934), 27; Younger, "Along The Way - Equality Versus Protection;" J. Stanley Lemons, The Woman Citizen: Social Feminism in the 1920s (Urbana and Chicago: University of Illinois Press, 1973), 202-203; New York Times, 28 June 1936.

19.   Labor Clarion, 21 June 1912; Chronicle, 1 March 1912; Louis S. Lyons, ed. Who's Who Among the Women of California (San Francisco: Security Publishing Co., 1922), 503. Rebecca Mead deftly documents the fuller story of the unionization of women in San Francisco and their resultant political activity, demonstrating that detailed research in local newspapers and union records can uncover something of the lives of women like O'Donnell and LaRue. Mead, "Trade Unionism and Political Activity Among San Francisco Wage-Earning Women, 1900-1922."

20.   Minna O'Donnell, former printer and ITU activist, may have also played a similar role. Because more is not known about her, one can only speculate about her status in the WESL.

21.   At some level, her relationship with labor may also have been Younger's attempt to find her niche for herself as a member of this community. She seemed at home fraternizing with the delegates at boisterous Labor Council meetings, socializing with the Waitresses' Union members at the hall and speaking for the rights of union and wage-earning women. While a suffragist, she felt uneasy with the class superiority insinuated or expressed by reformers in the movement.

22.   Considering Elinor Langer's assertion about New York City Irish hostility towards woman suffrage ballot referenda, this was an accomplishment. Langer found that while Jewish and some Italian neighborhoods went for suffrage, many Irish districts opposed enfranchising women. Many of these districts cast seventy to eighty-four percent of their vote cast against woman suffrage. Langer cited the Irish community's gender-segregated nature and conservative trade union tradition as the causes. San Francisco provides a much different picture. Elinor Langer, "Family Structure, Occupational Patterns, and Support for Women's Suffrage," in Women in Culture and Politics: A Century of Change, ed. Judith Friedlander, Blanche Wiesen-Cook, and others. (Bloomington: Indiana University Press, 1986), 223-236.

23.   For sources on the New York WESL, see the Leonora O'Reilly Papers, Arthur and Elizabeth Schlesinger Library on the History of Women in America, Radcliffe College, Cambridge, Mass; Rose Schneiderman Papers, Tamiment Institute Library, New York University, New York, NY; National Women's Trade Union League Papers, Manuscripts Division, Library of Congress, Washington, D.C.   Sources on the Chicago WESL include Women's Trade Union League of Chicago Records, 1908-1922, Special Collections, University Library, University of Illinois at Chicago, Chicago, Ill.   In New York and Chicago, WESLs formed as part of NWTUL chapters.   In Los Angeles, where Frances Noel established an NWTUL branch after the suffrage campaign, the WESL chapter emerged from the leadership of the Steam Laundry Workers' Local 36 and other women unionists and union auxiliary members active in the Los Angeles Central Labor Council.   Many of these women were in the Socialist Party.   Katz, "Frances Nacke Noel and 'Sister Movements,'"182-184.

SELECTED BIBLIOGRAPHY

Manuscript Collections

Minerva Goodman Papers, Holt-Atherton Center for Western History, University of the Pacific, Stockton, CA.

Keith-Pond-McHenry Papers. Bancroft Library. University of California, Berkeley, CA.

Ann Martin Papers. Bancroft Library. University of California, Berkeley, CA.

San Francisco Labor Council Manuscript Collection. Bancroft Library. University of California, Berkeley, CA.

Inez Haynes Irwin Papers. The Arthur and Elizabeth Schlesinger Library on the History of Women in America. Radcliffe College, Cambridge, MA.

Citizens League for Justice Papers. University Research Library. University of California, Los Angeles, CA.

Frances Noel Papers. University Research Library. University of California, Los Angeles, CA.

Alice L. Park Papers. Huntington Library. San Marino, CA.

National Women's Party Papers. Library of Congress. Washington, D.C.

National Women's Trade Union League Papers. Library of Congress. Washington, D.C.

Sophia Smith Collection, Suffrage-U.S. Biography Subject Collection, Smith College, Northampton, MA.

Newspapers and Periodicals

Mixer and Server

San Francisco Bulletin

San Francisco Call

San Francisco Chronicle

San Francisco. Coast Seamen's Journal

San Francisco Daily News

San Francisco Examiner

San Francisco Labor Clarion

San Francisco. The Leader

San Francisco. The Liberator

San Francisco. The Monitor

San Francisco. Organized Labor

San Francisco. Revolt

Government Publications

San Francisco. Board of Supervisors. San Francisco Municipal Reports. San Francisco: Neal Publishing Co., 1908-1917.

State of California. Bureau of Labor Statistics. Fifteenth Biennial Report, 1911-1912. Sacramento: State Printing Office,1912.

State of California. Secretary of State. Elections and Political Reform Division. General Election Returns, 3 November 1896. California State Archives, Sacramento, CA.

State of California. Secretary of State. Statement of the Vote of California at the Special Election Held on October 10, 1911 on Constitutional Amendments. Sacramento: Superintendent of State Printing, 1911

U.S. Bureau of the Census. Department of Commerce. Fourteenth Census of the United States: 1920. 11 vols. Washington, D.C.: Government Printing Office, 1922-23.

U.S. Bureau of the Census. Department of Commerce and Labor. Thirteenth Census of the United States: 1910. 11 vols. Washington, D.C.: U.S. Government Printing Office, 1914.

U.S. Bureau of the Census. Department of Commerce and Labor. Thirteenth Census of the United States: 1910, Abstract of the Census with Supplement for California. Washington, D.C.: Government Printing Office, 1913.

U.S. Census Office. Department of the Interior. Eleventh Census of the United States: 1890. 15 vols., compendium. Washington, D.C.: U.S. Government Printing Office, 1892.

U.S. Census Office. Department of the Interior. Twelfth Census of the United States: 1900. 37 vols. Washington, D.C.: U.S. Government Printing Office, 1902-1904.

Books and Articles

Anthony, Susan B. and Ida Husted Harper, eds. The History of Woman Suffrage, vol. 4-6. New York: National American Woman Suffrage Association, 1922.

Balser, Diane. Sisterhood and Solidarity. Boston: South End Press, 1987.

Blair, Karen. The Clubwoman as Feminist. New York: Holmes and Meier, Publishers, Inc., 1980.

Blatch, Harriot Stanton and Alma Lutz. Challenging the Years: The Memoirs of Harriot Stanton Blatch. New York: G.P. Putnam and Sons, 1940.

Boone, Gladys. The Women's Trade Union League in Great Britain and the United States of America. New York: Columbia Press, 1942.

Cantor, Milton and Bruce Laurie, eds. Class, Sex and the Woman Worker. Westport, Conn.: Greenwood Press, 1979.

Cherny, Robert W. and William Issel. San Francisco: Presidio, Port and Pacific Metropolis. San Francisco: Boyd and Fraser, 1981.

Cobble, Dorothy Sue. "'Practical Women': Waitress Unionists and the Controversies Over Gender Roles in the Food Service Industry, 1900-1980." Labor History 29 (Winter 1988): 15-23.

Cobble, Dorothy Sue. "Rethinking Troubled Relations Between Women and Unions: Craft Unionism and Female Activism." Feminist Studies 16 (Fall 1990): 519-548

College Equal Suffrage League of Northern California. Winning Equal Suffrage in California. College Equal Suffrage League of Northern California, n.d.

Cott, Nancy F. The Grounding of Modern Feminism. New Haven, Yale University Press, 1987.

Cross, Ira B. A History of the Labor Movement of California. Berkeley: University of California Press, 1935.

Dickinson, Joan Younger. The Role of the Immigrant Woman in the United States Labor Force, 1890-1910. New York: Arno Press, 1980.

Diner, Hasia R. Erin's Daughters in America. Baltimore: Johns Hopkins University Press, 1983.

DuBois, Ellen, Gerda Lerner, and others. "Politics and Culture in Women's History: A Symposium." Feminist Studies 6 (Spring 1980): 28-36

DuBois, Ellen. "Working Women, Class Relations, and Suffrage Militance: Harriot Stanton Blatch and the New York Woman Suffrage Movement, 1894-1909." Journal of American History 74 (June 1987): 34-58.

Dye, Nancy Schrom. As Equals and As Sister: Feminism, Unionism and the Women's Trade Union League of New York. Columbia: University of Missouri Press, 1980.

Eaves, Lucile. A History of California Labor with an Introductory Sketch of the San Francisco Labor Movement. University of California Publications in Economics, vol. 2. Berkeley: University of California Press, 1910.

Edmundson, Vera. "Feminist and Laborite." Sunset Magazine (June 1915): 1179-1180.

Eisenstein, Sarah. Give Us Bread, But Give Us Roses: Working Women's Consciousness in the United States, 1890 to World War I. London: Routledge & Kegan Paul, 1983.

Flexner, Eleanor. Century of Struggle. Cambridge: Belknap Press, 1959; New York: Atheneum, 1973.

Foner, Phillip. Women and the American Labor Movement, 2 vols. New York: The Free Press, 1979.

Greenwald, Maureen Weiner. "Working-Class Feminism and the Family Wage Ideal: The Seattle Debate on Married Women's Right to Work." Journal of American History 76 (June 1989): 118-149.

Gullett, Gayle. "City Mothers, City Daughters, and the Dance Hall Girls: The Limits of Female Political Power in San Francisco, 1913," in Women and the Structure of Society: Selected Research from the Fifth Berkshire Conference on the History of Women, ed. Barbara J. Harris and Joann K. McNamera, 149-159. Durham, N.C.: Duke University Press, 1984.

Issel, William and Robert W. Cherny. San Francisco, 1865-1932: Politics, Power and Urban Development. Berkeley and Los Angeles: University of California Press, 1986.

James, Edward T., Janet Wilson James and Paul S. Boyer, eds. Notable American Women, 1607-1950, 3 vols. Cambridge: Belknap Press, 1971.

Jensen, Joan M. and Gloria R. Lothrup. California Women: A History. San Francisco: Boyd and Fraser Publishing Co., 1987.

Katz, Sherry. "Frances Nacke Noel and 'Sister Movements': Socialism, Feminism and Trade Unionism in Los Angeles, 1909-1916." California History 67 (September 1988): 181-189, 207-210.

Kazin, Michael. Barons of Labor: The San Francisco Building Trades and Union Power in the Progressive Era. Urbana and Chicago: University of Illinois Press, 1986.

Kerber, Linda K. and Jane DeHart-Matthews. Woman's America. New York: Oxford University Press, 1982.

Kessler-Harris, Alice. Out to Work. New York: Oxford University Press, 1982.

Knight, Robert Edward Lee. Industrial Relations in the San Francisco Bay Area,
    1900-1918. Berkeley and Los Angeles: University of California Press,
    1960.

Kraditor, Aileen S. The Ideas of the Woman Suffrage Movement. New York:
    Columbia University Press, 1965.

Link, Arthur S. and Richard L. McCormick. Progressivism. Arlington Heights,
    Ill.: Harlan Davidson, Inc., 1983.

London, Jack. "South of the Slot." in Strength of the Strong. New York: The
    Macmillan Co., 1919.

Matthews, Lillian Ruth. Women in Trade Unions in San Francisco. University
    of California Publications in Economics, vol. 3. Berkeley: University of
    California Press, 1913.

May, Elaine Tyler. "Expanding the Past: Recent Scholarship on Women in
    Politics and Work." Reviews in American History 10 (December 1982):
    216-233.

Meyerowitz, Joanne J. Women Adrift: Independent Wage Earners in Chicago,
    1880-1930. Chicago: University of Chicago Press, 1988.

Mowry, George E. The California Progressives. Berkeley: University   of
    California Press, 1951.

Mitchell, Juliet and Ann Oakley, eds. What Is Feminism? New York: Pantheon
    Books, 1986.

National American Woman Suffrage Association. Woman Suffrage: Arguments
    and Results, 1910-1911. New York: National American Woman Suffrage
    Association, 1911; New York: Kraus Reprint Co., 1971.

Ostrander, Gilman M. The Prohibition Movement in California, 1848- 1933.
    University of California Publications in History, vol. 57. Berkeley and
    Los Angeles: University of California Press, 1957.

Payne, Elizabeth Anne. Reform, Labor and Feminism: Margaret Dreier Robins
    and the Women's Trade Union League. Urbana and Chicago: University
    of Illinois Press, 1988.

Peiss, Kathy. Cheap Amusements: Working Women and Leisure in Turn-of-the-Century New York. Philadelphia: Temple University Press, 1986.

Peixotto, Jessica B. "Women of California as Trade Unionists." Publications of the Association of Collegiate Alumnae, 3 (December 1908): 40-49.

Reverby, Susan. "The Labor and Suffrage Movements: A View of Working-Class Women in the Twentieth Century." in Liberation Now, 94-101. New York: Dell Publishing Co., 1971.

Saxton, Alexander. The Indispensible Enemy: Labor and the Anti-Chinese Movement in San Francisco. Berkeley and Los Angeles: University of California Press, 1971.

Schaffer, Ronald. "The Problem of Consciousness in the Woman Suffrage Movement: A California Perspective." Pacific Historical Review 45 (November 1976): 469-493.

Schofield, Ann. "Rebel Girls and Union Maids: The Woman Question in the Journals of the AFL and IWW, 1905-1920." Feminist Studies 9 (Summer 1983): 335-358.

Solomons, Selina. How We Won the Vote in California: A True Story of the Campaign of 1911. San Francisco: The New Woman Publishing Co., n.d.

Tax, Meredith. The Rising of the Women. New York: Monthly Review Press, 1980.

Tentler, Leslie Woodcock. Wage-Earning Women: Industrial Women and Family Life in the United States, 1900-1930. New York: Oxford University Press, 1979.

Tygiel, Jules. "'Where Unionism Holds Undisputed Sway'- A Reappraisal of San Francisco's Union Labor Party." California History 62 (Fall 1983): 196-215.

Weiner, Lynn. From Working Girl to Working Mother: The Female Labor Force in the United States, 1820-1980. Chapel Hill: University of North Carolina Press, 1985.

Wertheimer, Barbara M. We Were There: The Story of Working Women in America. New York: Pantheon Books, 1977.

Wiebe, Robert. The Search for Order, 1877-1920. New York: Hill and Wang, 1967.

Younger, Maud. "The Diary of an Amateur Waitress: An Industrial Problem from the Worker's Point of View." McClure's Magazine (March, April 1907): 542-552, 665-677.

Younger, Maud. "Taking Orders." Sunset Magazine (October 1908): 518-522.

Unpublished Works

Breen, Nancy. "Did San Francisco Women Unionists Choose the Wrong Benchmark?" Paper presented at the Southwest Labor Studies Association annual meeting, Stockton, CA, March, 1991.

Cobble, Dorothy Sue. "Sisters in the Craft: Waitresses and Their Unions in the Twentieth Century." Ph.D. dissertation, Stanford University, 1986.

Crockett, Earl C. "History of California Labor Legislation, 1910- 1930." Ph.D. dissertation, University of California, Berkeley, 1931.

Eaves, Edward P. "A History of the Cooks' and Waiters' Unions of San Francisco." M.A. thesis, University of California, Berkeley, 1930.

Ethington, Philip J. "Gender, Class, and Privilege: The Contested Terrain of Political Culture in San Francisco, 1890-1920." Paper presented at the American Historical Association annual meeting, 27-30 December 1989.

Grey, Barbara L. "One Woman's Struggle." Independent Study, City College of San Francisco, 1988.

Hicke, Carole. "The 1911 Campaign of James Rolph, Jr., Mayor of All the People." M.A. thesis, San Francisco State University, 1978.

Katz, Sherry. "Frances Noel and the Working Class Woman: Female Solidarity and Class Consciousness in Los Angeles, 1909-1916." Seminar paper, University of California, Los Angeles, 1985.

Kazin, Michael. "Barons of Labor: The San Francisco Building Trades, 1896-1922." Ph.D. dissertation, Stanford University, 1983.

Mead, Rebecca J. "Trade Unionism and Political Activity Among San Francisco Wage-Earning Women, 1900-1922." M.A. thesis, San Francisco State University, 1991.

Ohlson, Robert Verner. "History of the San Francisco Labor Council, 1892-1937." Ph.D. dissertation, University of California, Berkeley, 1939.

Ploeger, Louise M. "Trade Unionism Among the Women of San Francisco, 1920." M.A. thesis, University of California, Berkeley, 1920.

Rodes, Daniel W. "The California Woman Suffrage Campaign of 1911." M.A. thesis, California State University at Hayward, 1974.

Rowell, Edward. "The Union Labor Party of San Francisco, 1901-1910." Ph.D. dissertation, University of California, Berkeley, 1928.

Shackelford, Ruth. "Trial By Fire: The California Woman Suffrage Campaign of 1911." Seminar paper, San Francisco State University, 1983.

Tygiel, Jules. "Workingmen in San Francisco 1880-1901." Ph.D. dissertation, University of California, Los Angeles, 1977.

INDEX

Amendment Eight (1911) 1, 2, 128, 130, 134-141, 153, 154, 171, 172

American Federation of Labor 67, 70, 119, 121, 124, 135, 166, 185

Anthony, Susan B. . . . 4, 10, 42, 54, 55, 66, 73, 75, 76, 81, 100, 101, 104, 181

Anti-Asian movement . 49-51, 168

Asiatic Exclusion League 50

Bindery Women Local 125 . . . 50

Blatch, Harriot Stanton . . . 6, 9, 10, 71, 113, 117, 118, 148, 149, 170, 175, 181, 182

Boot and Shoe Fitters' Protective Union 42

Calhoun, Patrick 82, 83, 106, 108

California Club 76-78, 89, 91, 101, 109, 115, 147

California Eight Hour Day Law for Women Workers . . 128-129

California Equal Suffrage Association (CESA) . 76, 77, 79, 92, 101, 109, 110, 119, 122, 126, 127, 130, 151, 156

California Federation of Labor 78, 97, 114, 120, 125, 126, 164, 168

California League of Women Voters 157

California Woman Suffrage Association 9, 73, 76

Catholic Church . . 17, 102, 156

Catt, Carrie Chapman . . . 76, 100

Century Club 77, 89, 101, 114, 118, 121, 147, 169

Chinese Exclusion Act 49

Civic League of California . . 157

Citizen's League of Justice (CLJ) . . . 89, 91, 92, 106-108

Club Women's Franchise League 130

Clubwomen 4, 77, 91, 101, 117, 132, 157, 163

Coast Seamen's Journal 51, 70, 93, 180

Coffin, Lillian Harris . . . . v, 77, 79, 87, 89, 90, 92, 107, 109, 114, 119, 129, 152

College Equal Suffrage League 127, 130, 135, 153, 154, 157, 172, 182

Congressional Union 149, 165, 175

Deering, Mabel 152

Democratic Party 95

Demographics 25-33
  Age 30-31
  Heads of Household 29
  Labor Participation
    Rates 26-27
  Marital Status . . . 30, 32-34
  "Women Adrift" . 27-29, 55

Domestic Code 25

Equal Rights Amendment . . . 166, 171, 175

Equality League for Self-Supporting Women 6, 117, 119

Ethnicity 17-25
  Black 20-21, 39
  Chinese 20-21, 39, 40
  German . . 17, 19, 20, 22, 24
  Irish 17-25, 26, 32, 43
  Italian . . . 17, 19, 20, 22, 24
  Japanese 20, 21, 39
  White foreign-born 21
  White native-born 21

Feminism . . ii, 6, 10-13, 15-17, 54, 57, 59-61, 72, 73, 99, 146, 155, 174-176, 182-184
  Working-class
    feminism . . . . ii, 6,10-13, 15-17, 54, 57,

Working-class
feminism *(cont)*
59-61, 72, 73, 99, 146,
155, 174-176, 182-184
Flynn, Elizabeth Gurley 97
French, Mrs. Will . 95, 117, 129
Gamage, Mary . . 77, 90, 92, 107
Gerberding, Elizabeth . 79, 89-92,
106, 107, 163
Hale, Sarah 81
Hart, Sallie 8, 9, 13, 75
Heney, Francis . . 91, 92, 94, 107
Humane Legislation
League 159, 160,
167, 169, 172
Johnson, Grove L. 78
Johnson, Hiram . . 102, 128, 154
Keith, Mary McHenry 75, 77-79,
91, 99-101, 106-108, 127, 136,
141, 143, 145, 149, 151, 152,
154-156, 179
Kennedy, Kate . 6, 11, 12, 41, 42
Knights of Labor . 42, 55, 67, 71
Knights of the Royal Arch . . 141
Labor Clarion . . . 44, 52, 68-70,
80, 93, 95, 102-105, 108, 109,
114-118, 120, 121, 125, 126,
129, 130, 134, 136, 143, 146,
147-154, 157, 158, 171, 174,
176, 180
Labor Day Parade of 1909 . . 124
Labor Day Parade of 1911 134-136
Labor movement . . 2, 3, 11, 16,
43, 48, 50-52, 56, 62, 67,
69-73, 80, 85, 103, 108, 113,
159, 165, 166, 175, 176, 182,
183
Labor press . 16, 48, 51, 70, 122
LaRue, Louise 15, 47, 50,
58, 78, 80, 85-87, 94-98, 103,
114-117, 119, 120, 122, 124,
127-134, 151-153, 167, 169,
171, 172, 176
Laughlin, Gail . . . . . v, 76, 100

Lewis, Augusta 54, 55
Lincoln-Roosevelt League . . 128
London, Jack 12, 41, 66, 183, 184
MacDonald, Laura 123, 131
Mahoney, Hannah 45, 125
Matthews, Lillian . . . 7, 12, 23,
42, 44-46, 48, 50-52, 57, 62,
67-71, 73, 81, 82, 103-105,
183, 184
McCarthy, P.H. . . . 16, 49, 58,
68, 93, 94, 124, 129, 134, 137,
147, 148, 153, 157, 173
Mother Jones 80, 103
Muller v. Oregon 129
Myears, Rose 50, 125
National American Woman Suffrage
Association 9, 10,
73, 74, 76, 99, 100, 119, 122,
145, 181, 184
National Consumer's League . 55,
56, 71
National Women's Party 12, 100,
145, 153, 166, 167, 175, 179
National Women's Trade Union
League . . 50, 56, 69, 72, 95
102, 112, 124, 170, 177, 179
New Era Club 157
Newman, Pauline 57, 166
Noel, Frances . . . . . vii, 72, 73,
150, 151, 159, 160, 166, 169,
170, 174, 177, 179, 183, 186
Nolan, Hannah Mahoney . 45, 125
Nolan, John I. 97, 120, 129, 136
Occupations 33-41
Clerical 35, 37, 38, 39
Laundry Work . . 36, 38, 43,
45-56, 50-51, 81
Domestic and personal
services 33, 35-39
Industrial 35-39
Waitressing . . . 35, 36, 38,
43, 46-48, 50, 59
O'Donnell, Minna . v, 52, 94-96,
116-118, 124, 125, 127, 129,

O'Donnell, Minna *(cont)*
131, 149, 158, 167, 169, 172, 176
O'Reilly, Leonora 166, 177
Organized Labor . . . 40, 42, 50, 52, 53, 58, 67, 119, 123, 126, 134, 150, 151, 158, 160, 166, 167, 180
Park, Alice 77, 90, 92, 114, 122, 133, 135, 146, 179
Paul, Alice . . . . . . viii, 12, 66, 145, 165, 166, 174, 175, 183
Peet, Mrs. Sturtevant 75
Peixotto, Jessica 52, 185
Peterson, Agnes 41, 66
Ploeger, Louise 53, 70, 81, 82, 103, 104, 187
Progressive Era 3-5, 7, 8, 67, 77, 86, 108, 148, 173, 183
Racism 49-51, 169
Reform . . . . v, 2, 3, 8-10, 42, 58, 73, 74, 76, 78, 79, 82, 85, 87, 88, 91, 93-97, 111, 114, 119, 127, 142, 145, 146, 164, 166, 169-171, 180, 184
Republican Party 88, 128, 154, 157
Reynolds, Edith 124, 131
Rolph, James Jr. . 134, 153, 157, 173, 186
Ruef, Abraham 69, 88, 89, 91, 93, 94, 106, 108
San Francisco Board of Supervisors 61, 88
San Francisco Building Trades Council 16, 49, 52, 67, 68, 80, 93, 95, 105, 108, 124, 126, 150, 153, 159
San Francisco Council of Federated Trades 42
San Francisco Earthquake and Fire 109, 113
San Francisco Equal Suffrage League 74, 77, 78, 85, 92, 95-98, 109, 114, 127,

San Francisco Equal Suffrage League *(cont)*
130, 135, 154, 157, 169, 172, 182
San Francisco Graft Trials . . 109
San Francisco Labor Council . 2, 42, 48, 50-53, 58, 68, 69, 80, 83, 93, 95, 105, 108, 119, 124-126, 150, 158, 160, 163, 164, 168, 173, 174, 179, 187
San Francisco Wage Earners' Suffrage League . . . . v, vii, viii, 1-3, 7, 8, 16, 17, 58, 60, 95, 96, 98, 116-121, 129-132, 134, 135, 141, 168-172, 176, 177
Sargent, Ellen Clark . . . . . v, 55, 77, 79, 89, 90, 101
Schade, Cora 116
Scharrenberg, Elinor . . 125, 126
Schmitz, Eugene . . . 16, 68, 88, 89, 91, 104
Schneiderman, Rose 57, 72, 166, 177
Scott, Melinda 166
Solomons, Selina . . . 9, 101, 108, 109, 120, 127, 145, 149, 151, 158, 172, 173, 185
Sperry, Mary . . . . . . v, 55, 77, 79, 89, 90, 92, 109, 163
Stanton, Elizabeth Cady . . . 4, 6, 9, 10, 42, 54, 55, 71, 113, 117, 148, 149, 170, 175, 181, 182
Steam Laundry Workers' Union, Local 26 . . . . 48, 125, 131
Streetcar Strike of 1907 . . . 82-87
Class and 87
Conflict in woman suffrage movement over . . . 85-87
Women's participation . 84-85
Street Carmen's Union 82-84, 86
Telephone Operators' Union 114, 147
Temperance movement 79

Temperance movement *(cont)*
  Working-class response
    to 79-81
Twentieth Century Club 114, 118,
  121, 147, 169
Union Labor Party . . . 3, 16, 49,
  58, 68, 69, 78, 88, 90, 93, 94,
  97, 104, 106, 110, 124, 138,
  141, 147, 155, 157, 171, 173,
  185, 187
United Garment Workers, Local
  131 114
United Railroad 82, 89, 104, 108
Wage-earning women . 2, 3, 5-7,
  11, 12, 16, 20, 21, 25-31, 33,
  34, 43, 48, 54, 55, 57, 59,
  62-66, 71, 86, 115, 117,
  120-123, 127, 131, 132, 147,
  150, 163, 164, 166, 169-171,
  174, 176, 185, 187
  and Sexuality . 40, 110, 111
  and suffrage 1-2
  Demographics 25-33
  Ethnicity 17-25
  Labor segmentation 39
  Occupations 33-41
Waiters' Local 30 53
Waitresses' Union Local 48 . 15,
  17, 44, 46-48, 50, 53, 57-59,
  69, 78, 80, 81, 85, 94, 95,
  113-116, 118, 119, 121, 123,
  124, 126, 129, 131, 133, 150,
  167-171
Walden, L.C. 115, 125, 131
Watson, Elizabeth Lowe . 77, 127
Willard, Frances . 74, 75, 99, 100
Williams, Lizzie . . 125, 131, 148
Wilson, J. Stitt 127, 134,
  145, 174, 183
Woman Suffrage, History of ii, v,
  1-4, 6, 7, 9, 10, 12, 17, 42, 60,
  73-79, 90, 92, 95-102, 107-110,
  114, 116, 119-124, 128, 131,
  132, 134, 136, 137, 140-143,

Woman Suffrage, History of *(cont)*
  145, 149, 151, 152, 154-157,
  166, 168-170, 172, 175, 176,
  181, 182, 184, 187
  1896 California
    Campaign . . . 73-86, 77
  1911 California
    Campaign 1-2, 92
      109, 114, 128-143
  Historiography of 4-6
  Reform suffragists . . 76-79,
    89-92, 95, 96, 127
  San Francisco . . . 74, 76-78
    89, 92, 109, 116-117, 127,
    129-143
  Union suffragists . . 2-3, 6-8
    78, 85-86, 95-98, 122-123
  United States 54-60,
    73-74, 76, 119, 122, 127-
    128
Woman's Branch . 56, 89-92, 106
  Citizen's League of
    Justice 107
Women in Unions . 41-54, 81-82
  and Suffrage 54-60
  Female locals . . 2-3, 42, 44
    46-48, 53-54, 58-60
  Union membership . . . 42-60
Woman's Christian Temperance
  Union (WCTU) . 66, 74, 75,
  79, 91, 100
Women's Auxiliary #18,
  International Typographical
  Union 116,
    118, 124
Women's Cooperative Printing
  Union 41, 66
Women's Educational and Industrial
  Union 55, 71
Women's Municipal League . . 94
Women's Union Label
  League 124-127,
    151, 158, 159, 163, 169
  California . . . 121, 130, 159

Women's Union Label *(cont)*
  Los Angeles . . 121, 130, 159
  National organization . . . 121,
    130, 159
  San Francisco . 121, 130, 159
Woodward, Charlotte 54
Working Women's
  Association 54, 71
Workingmen's Party 49
Yorke, Father Peter . 43, 67, 83,
  141, 155, 156
Younger, Maud . . . . . . v, 2, 3,
  28, 96, 100, 110-120, 122, 123,
  125-128, 130-136, 145-147,
  149, 152, 153, 158, 165-167,
  169, 170, 171, 174-176, 182,
  186